HOW TO DRAW ANIMALS
Step By Step Drawing Book

This Book Belongs To

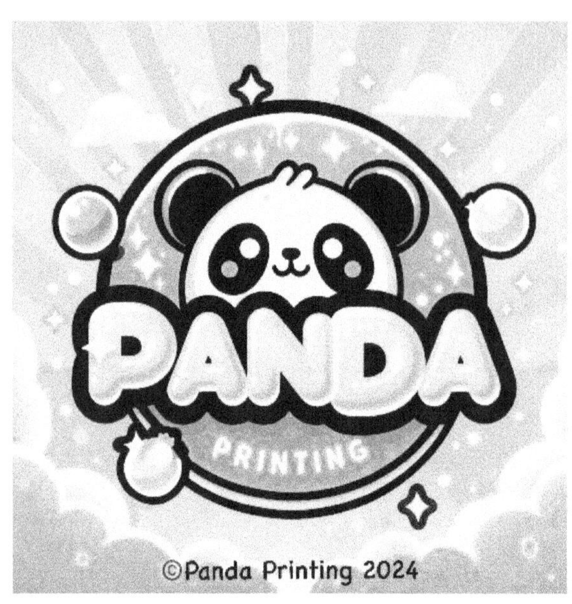

First published by Panda Printing 2024

Copyright © 2024 by Thomas Maxwell

First edition

Color Test Pages

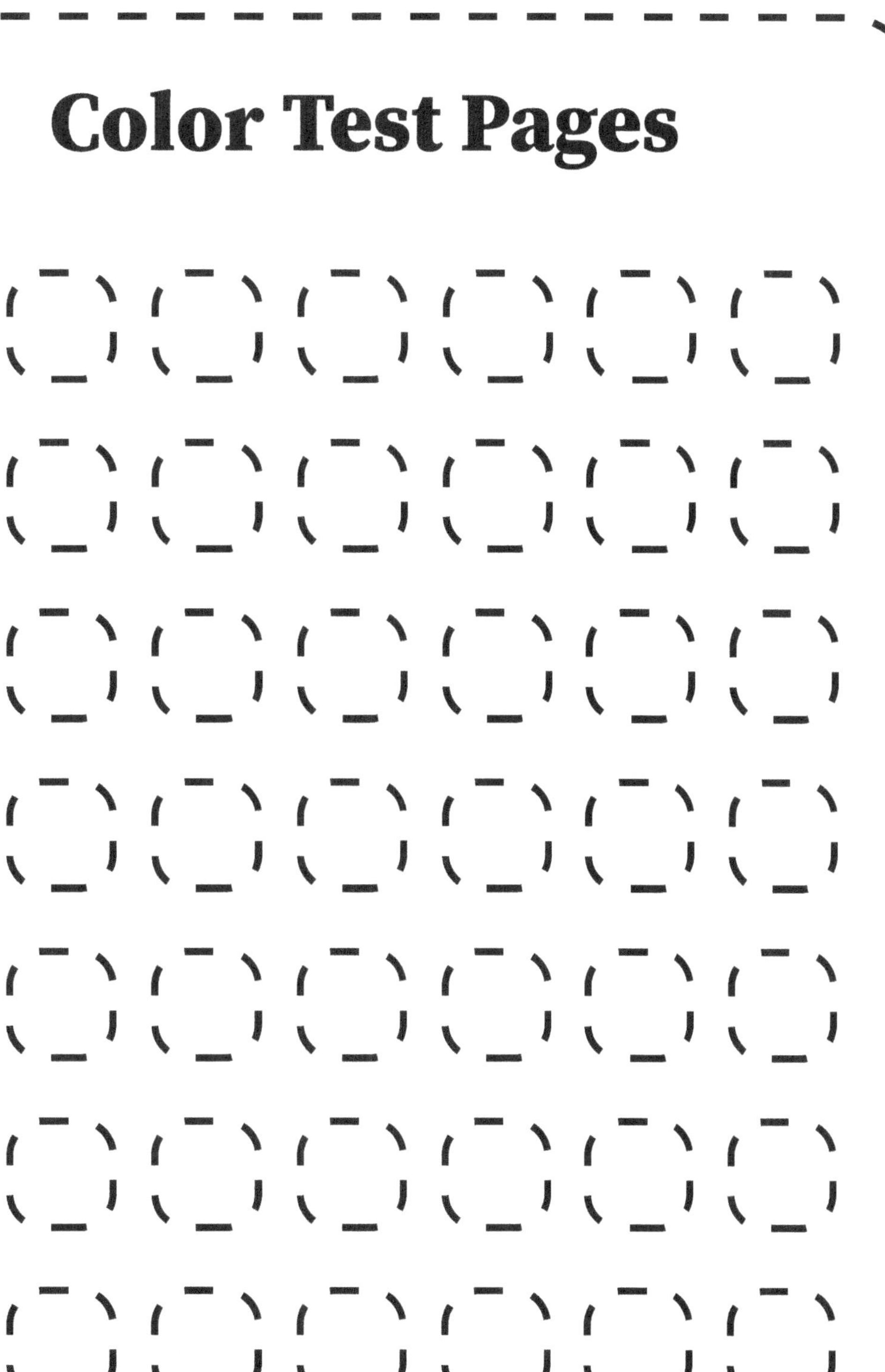

HOW TO DRAW

STEP - 1
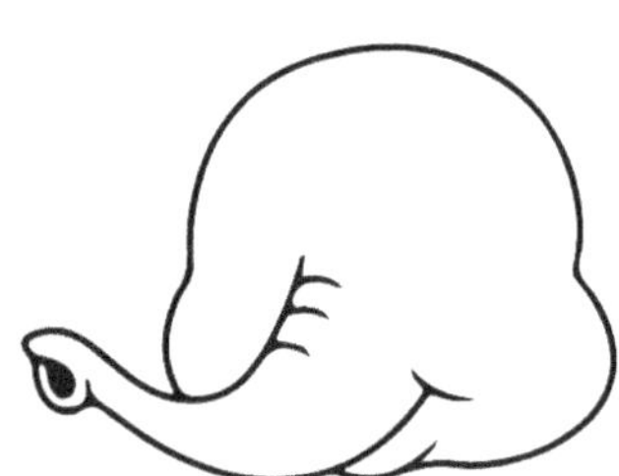

STEP - 2
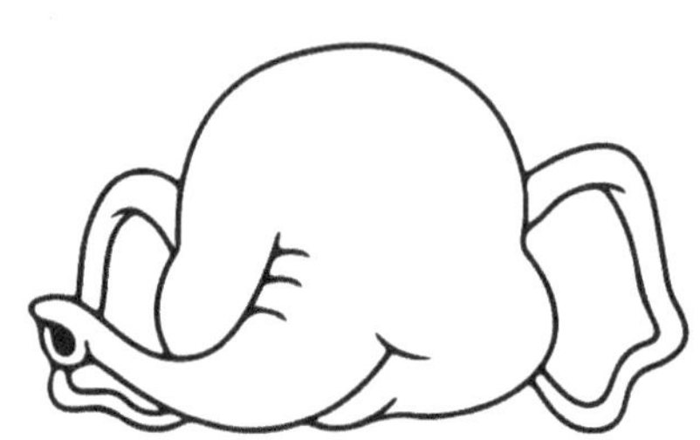

STEP - 3
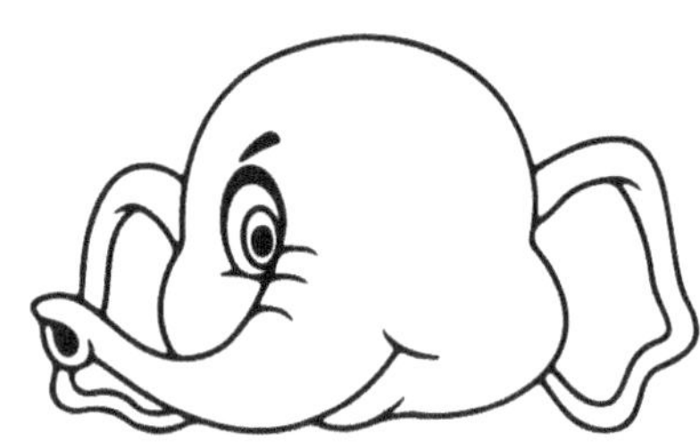

STEP - 4
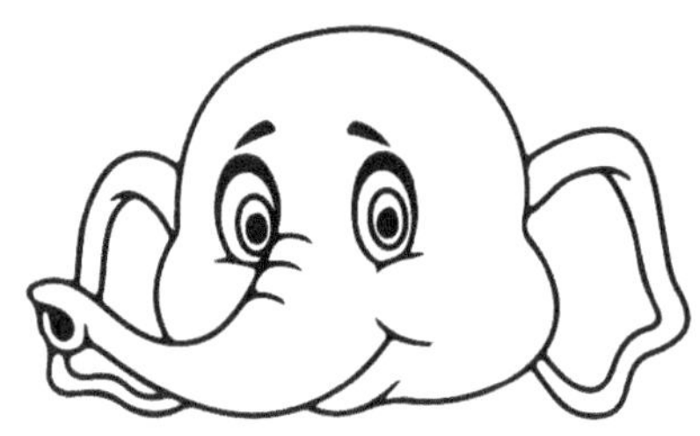

STEP - 5
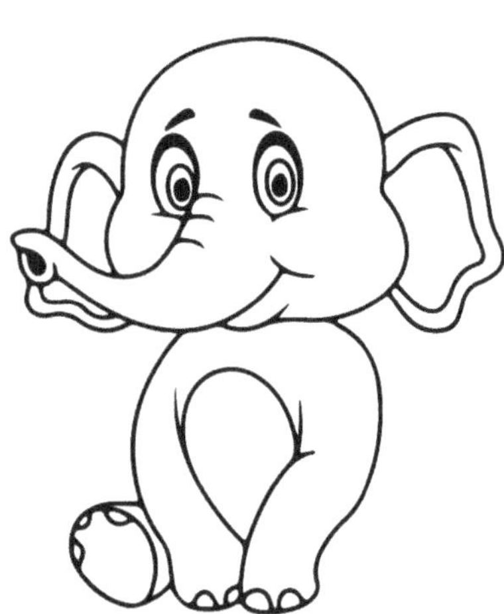

STEP - 6
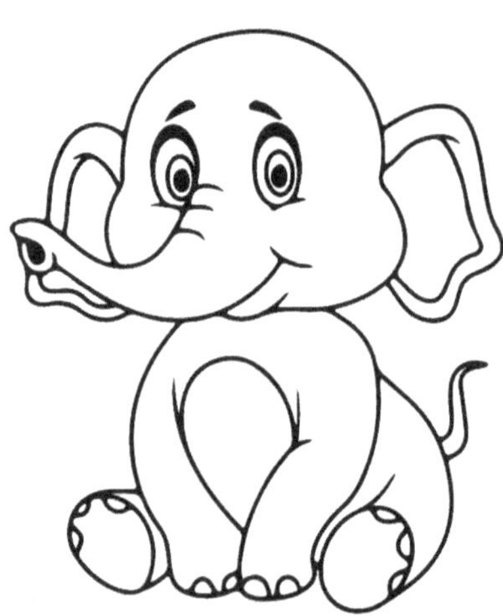

Your Test Pages

STEP - 1

STEP - 2

STEP - 3

STEP - 4

STEP - 5

STEP - 6

HOW TO DRAW

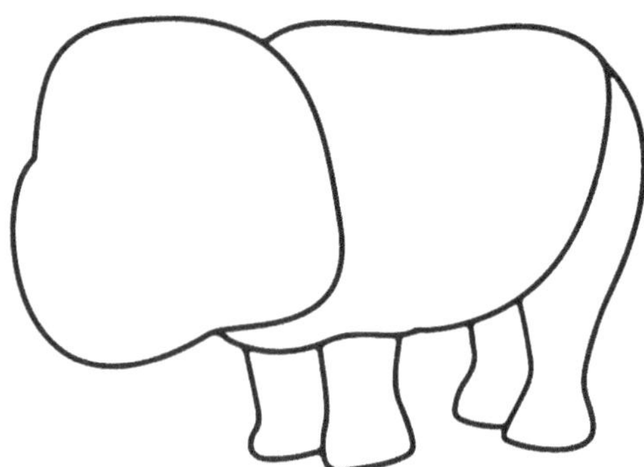

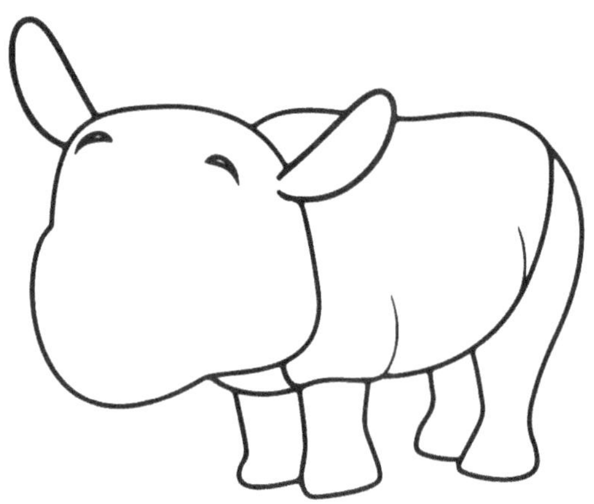

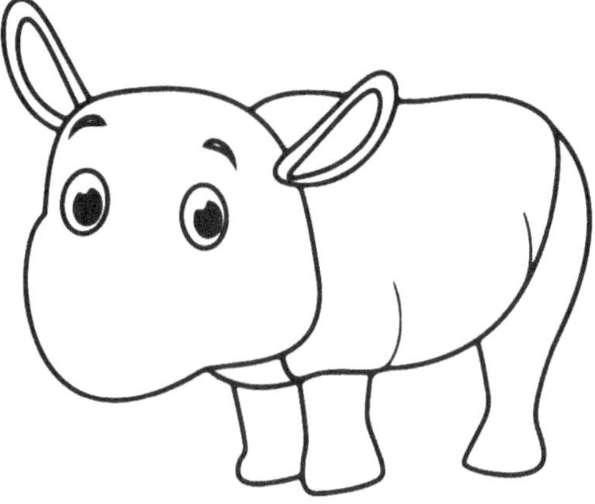

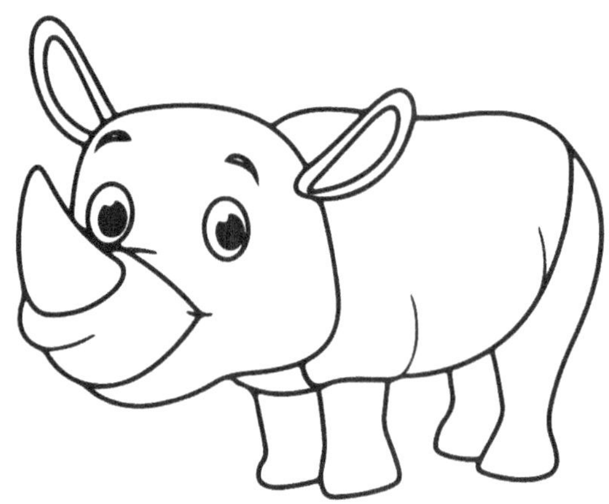

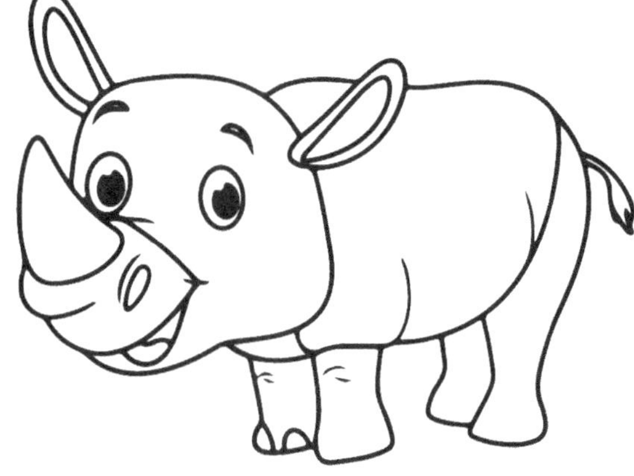

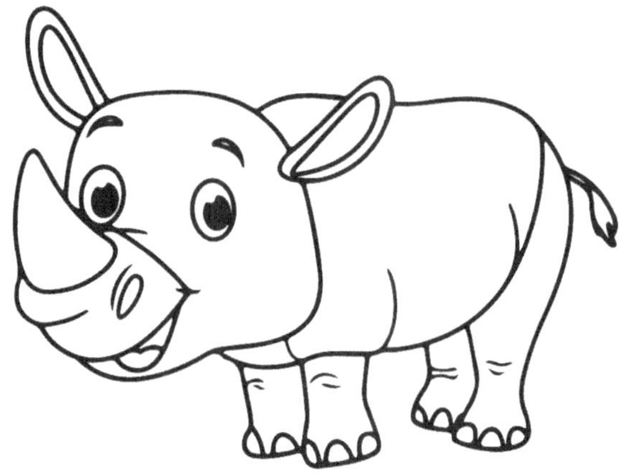

Your Test Pages

STEP - 1

STEP - 2

STEP - 3

STEP - 4

STEP - 5

STEP - 6

HOW TO DRAW

STEP - 1

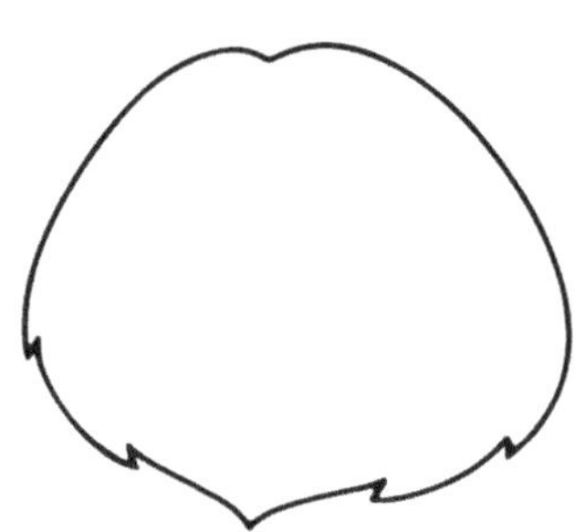

STEP - 2

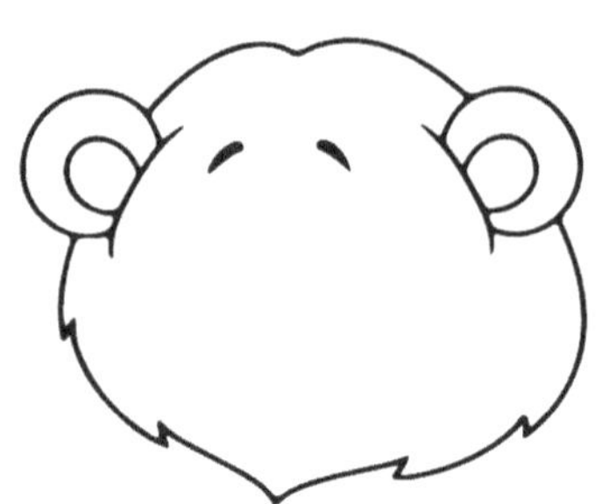

STEP - 3

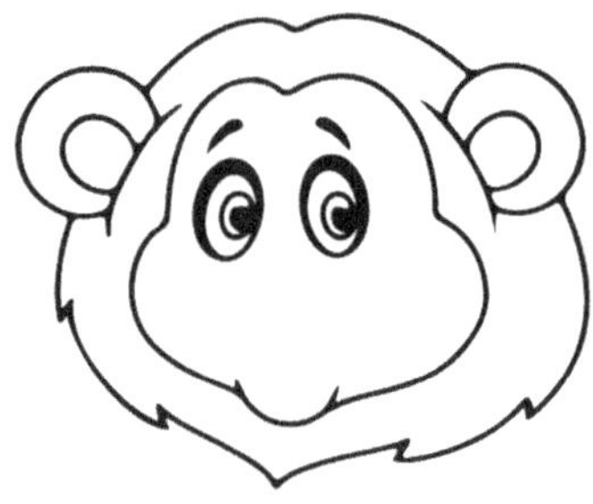

STEP - 4

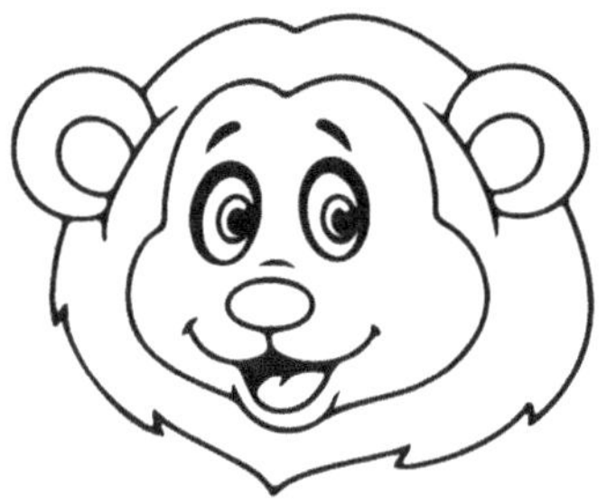

STEP - 5

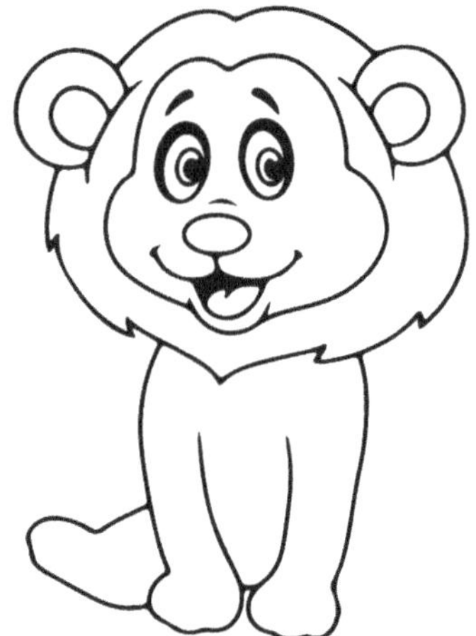

STEP - 6

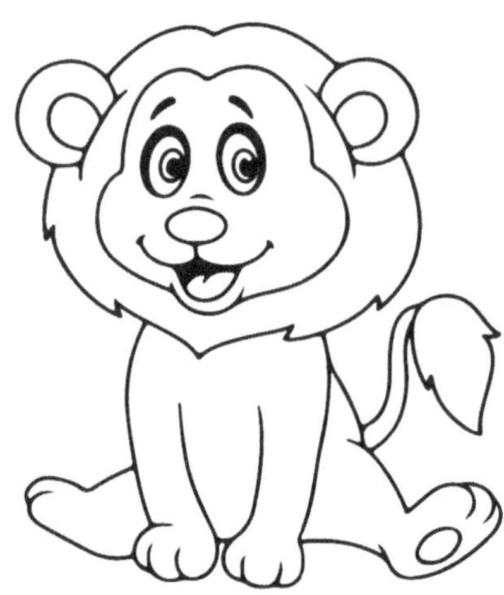

Your Test Pages

STEP - 1

STEP - 2

STEP - 3

STEP - 4

STEP - 5

STEP - 6

HOW TO DRAW

STEP - 1
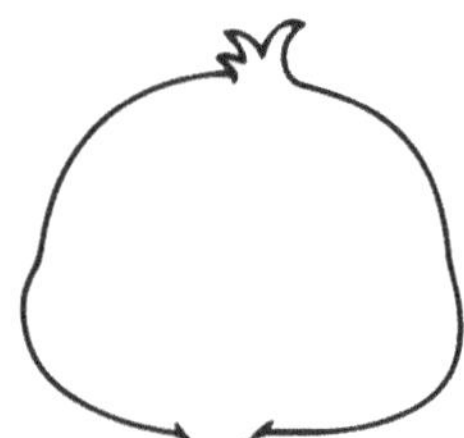

STEP - 2
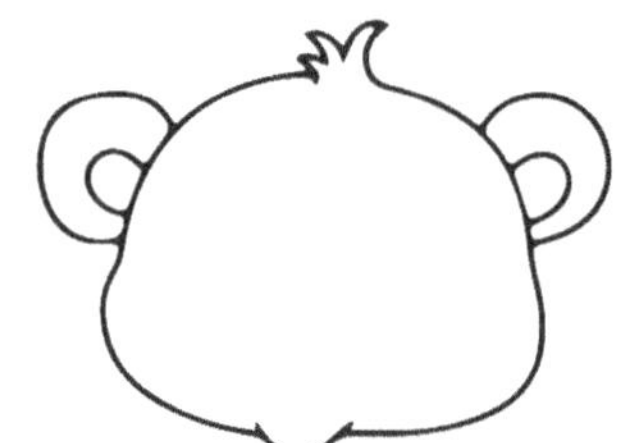

STEP - 3
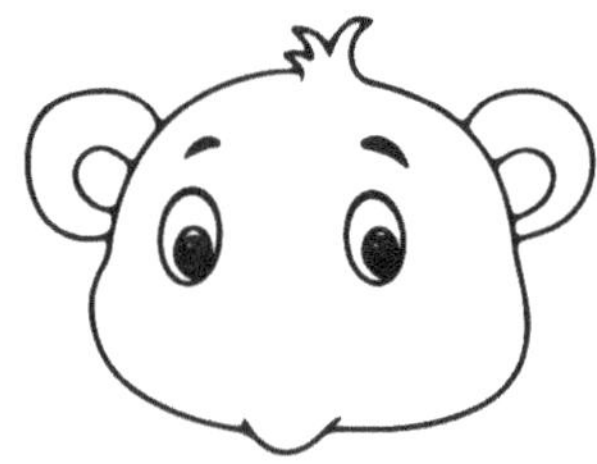

STEP - 4
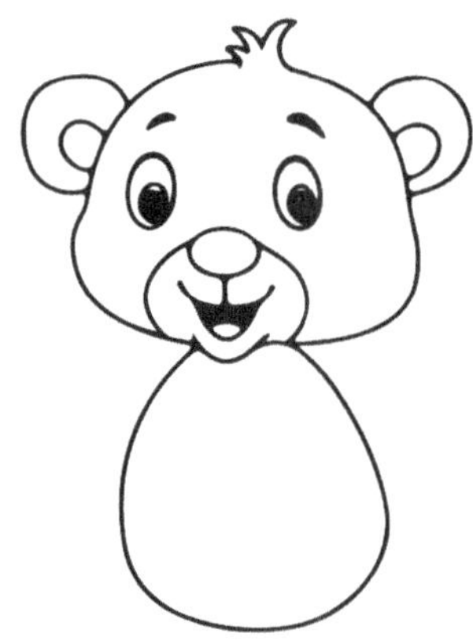

STEP - 5
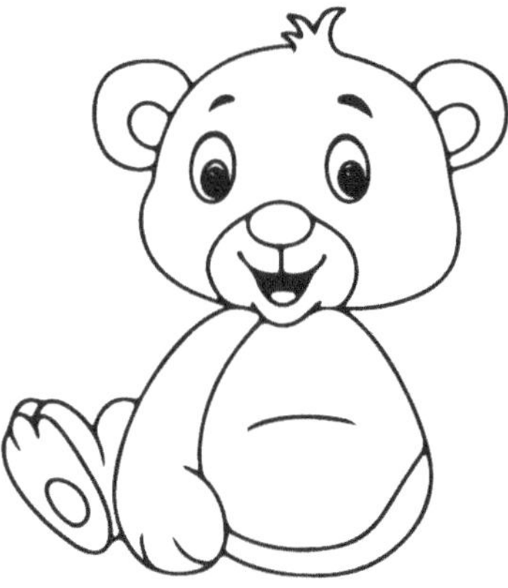

STEP - 6
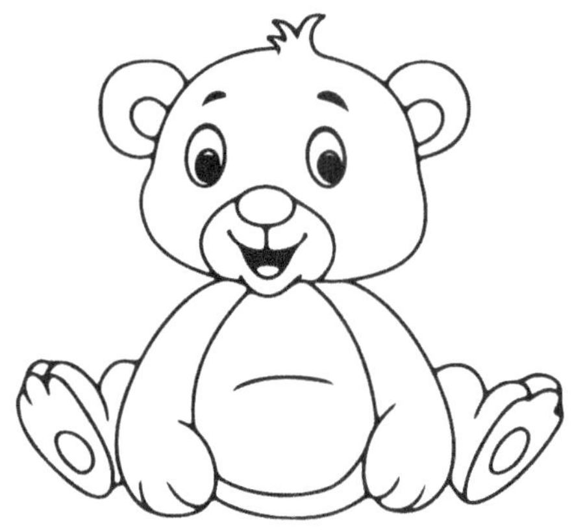

Your Test Pages

STEP - 1

STEP - 2

STEP - 3

STEP - 4

STEP - 5

STEP - 6

HOW TO DRAW

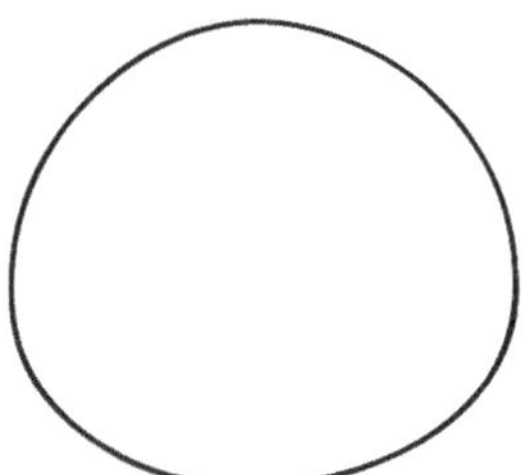

STEP - 1

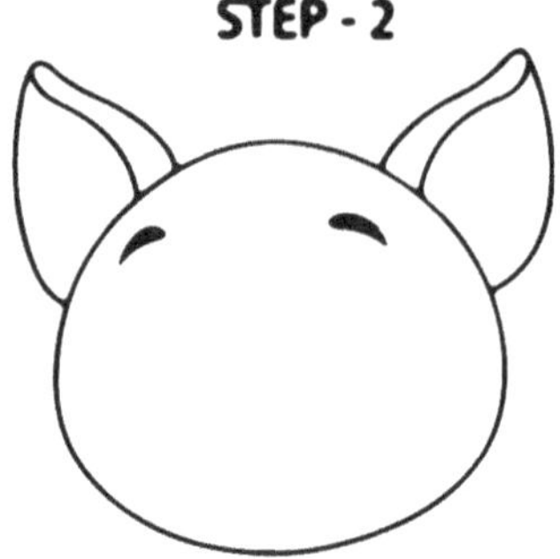

STEP - 2

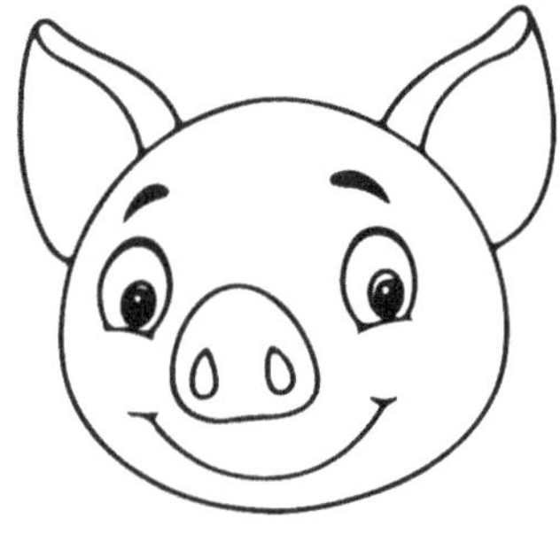

STEP - 3

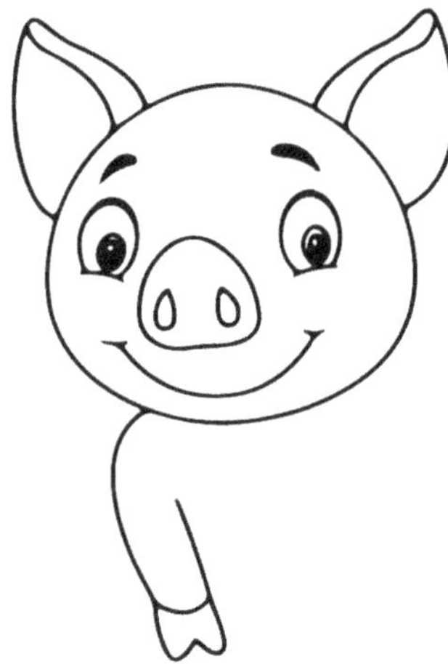

STEP - 4

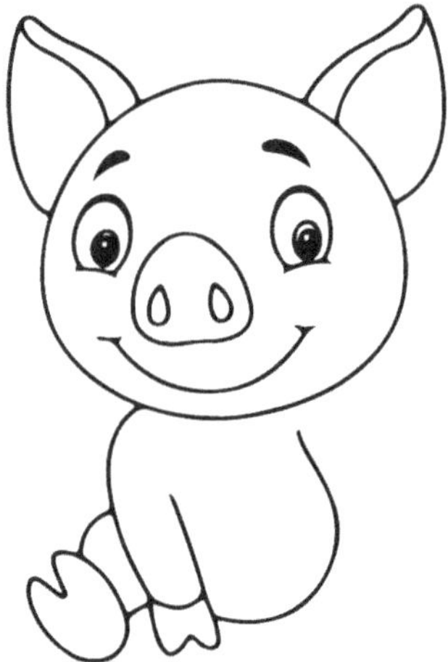

STEP - 5

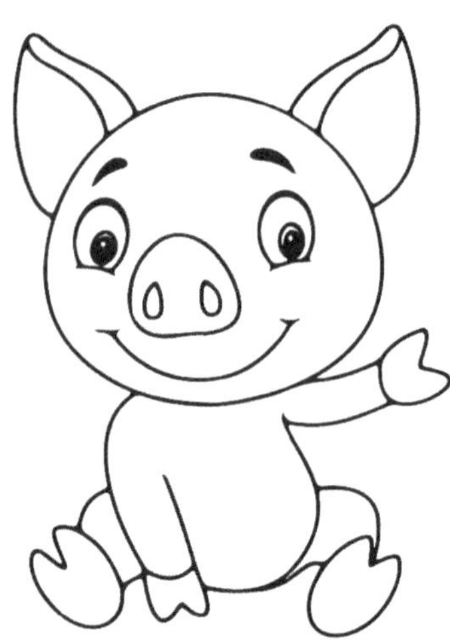

STEP - 6

Your Test Pages

STEP - 1

STEP - 2

STEP - 3

STEP - 4

STEP - 5

STEP - 6

HOW TO DRAW

STEP - 1

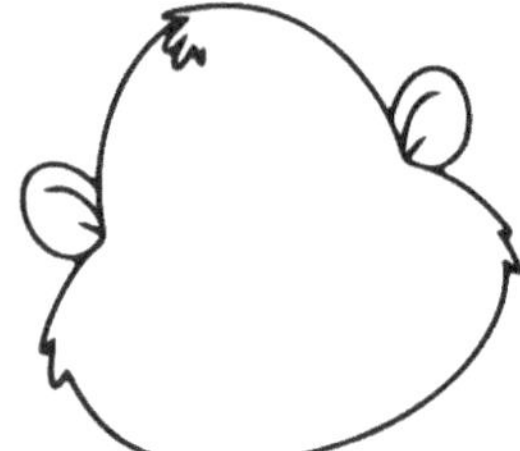

STEP - 2

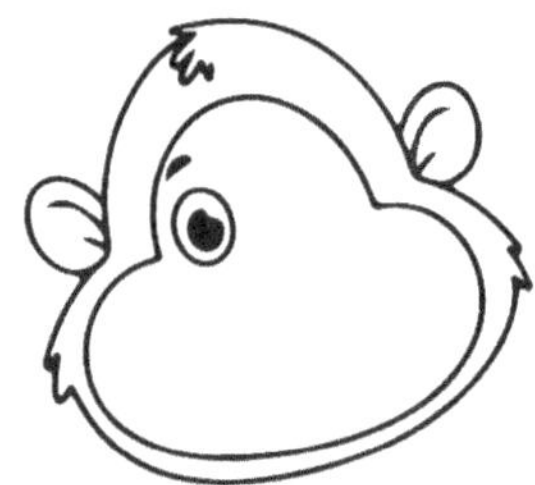

STEP - 3

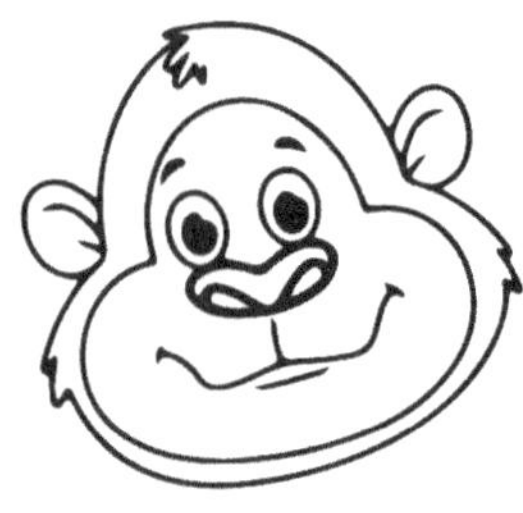

STEP - 4

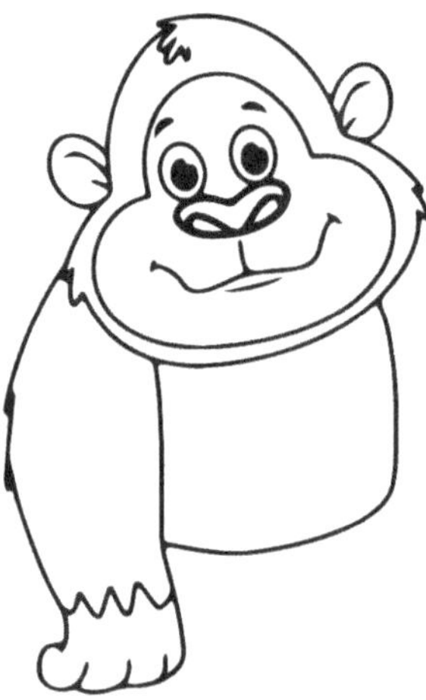

STEP - 5

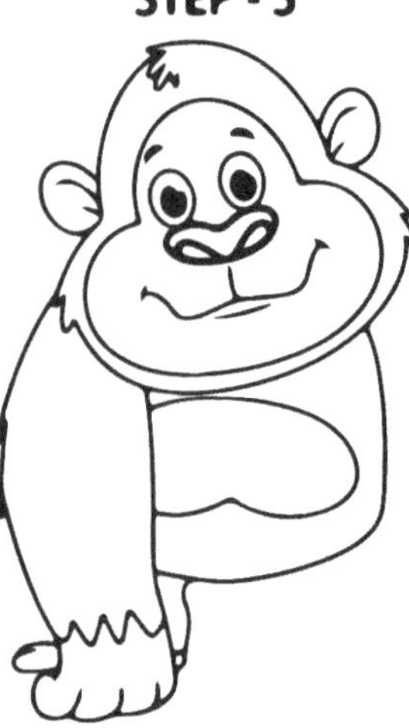

STEP - 6

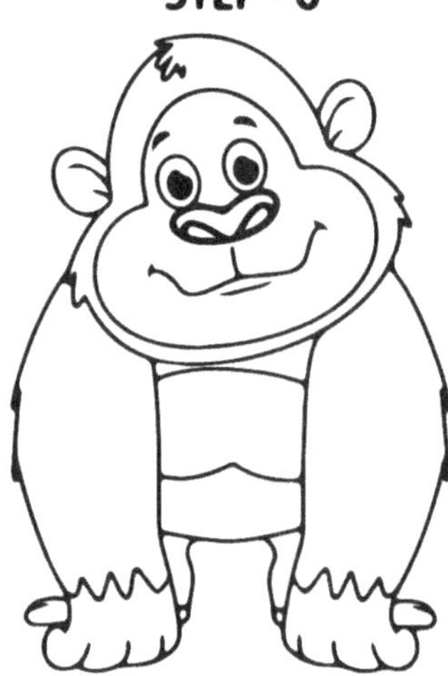

Your Test Pages

STEP - 1

STEP - 2

STEP - 3

STEP - 4

STEP - 5

STEP - 6

HOW TO DRAW

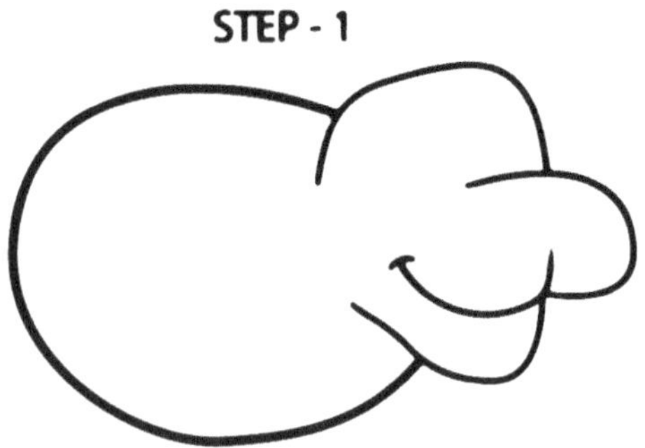

STEP - 1

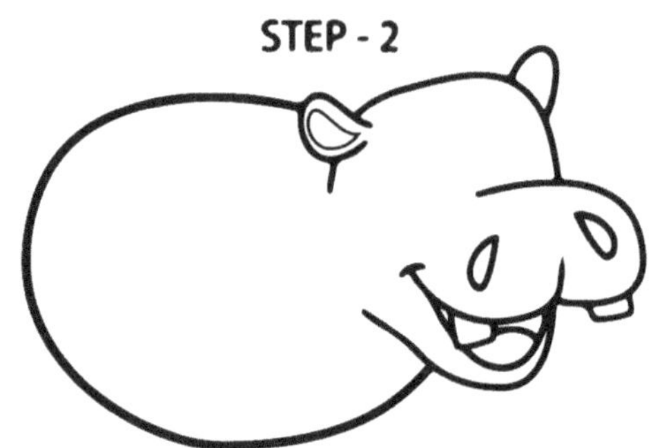

STEP - 2

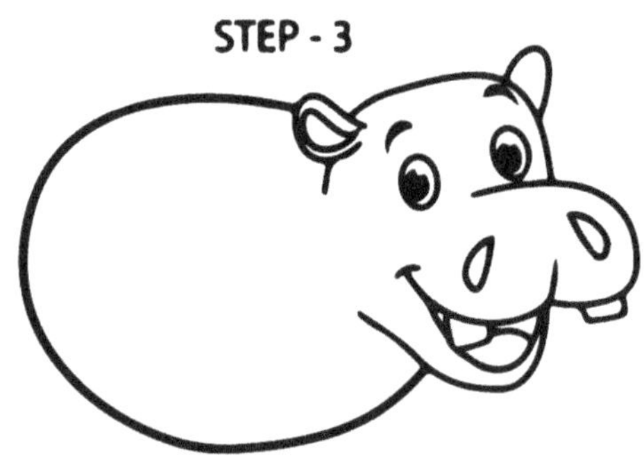

STEP - 3

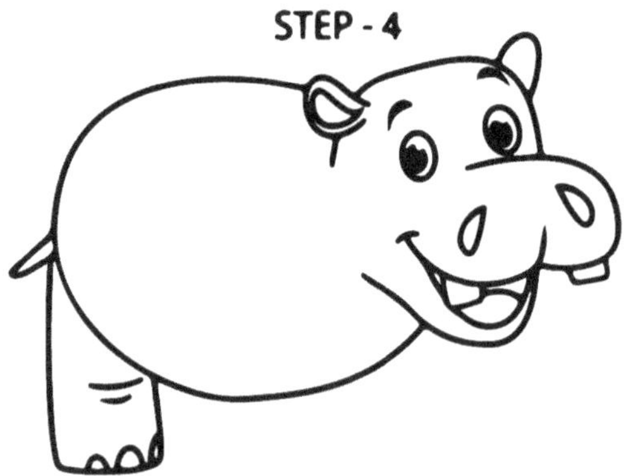

STEP - 4

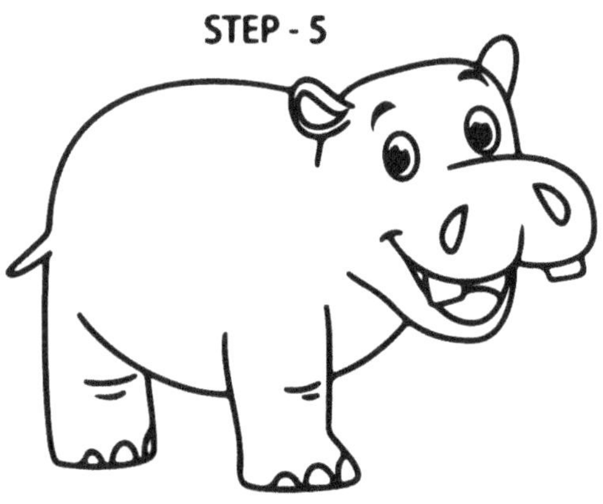

STEP - 5

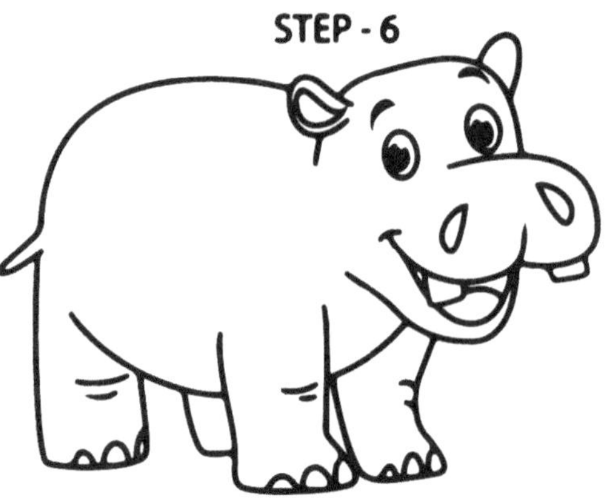

STEP - 6

STEP - 1

STEP - 2

STEP - 3

STEP - 4

STEP - 5

STEP - 6

HOW TO DRAW

STEP - 1

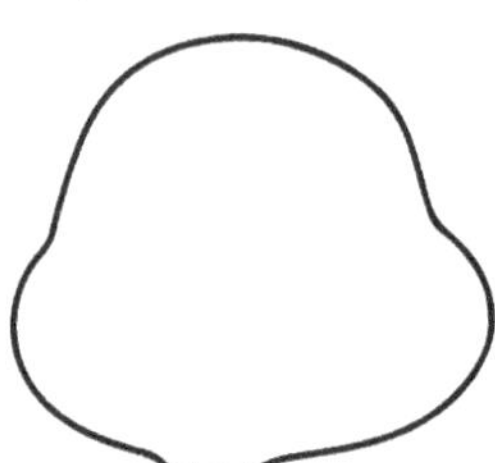

STEP - 2

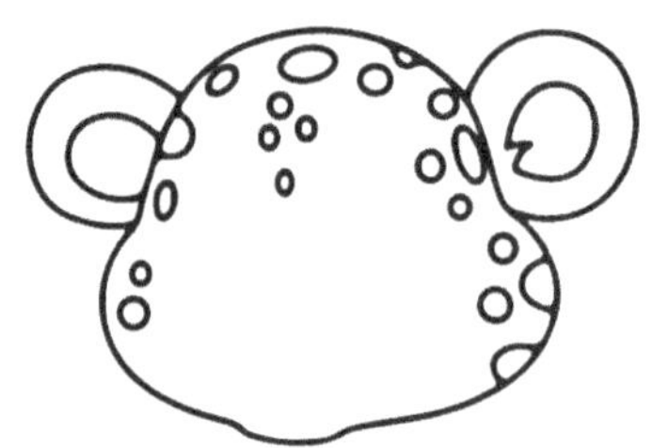

STEP - 3

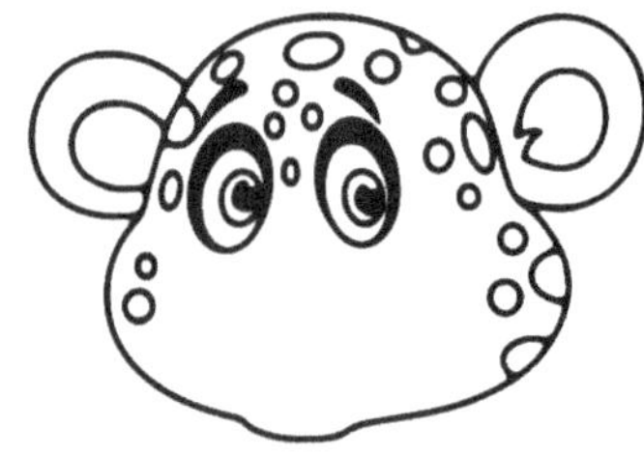

STEP - 4

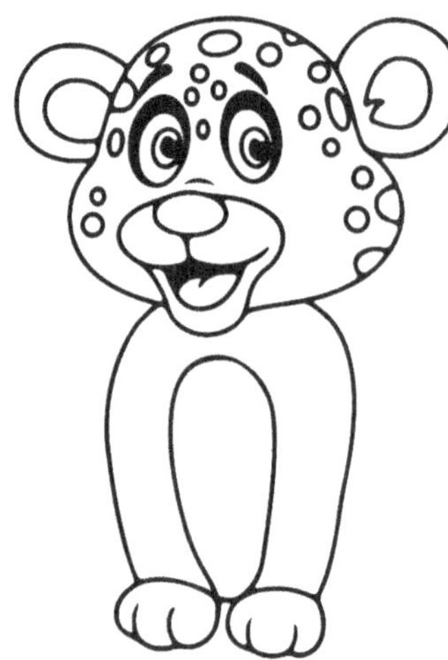

STEP - 5

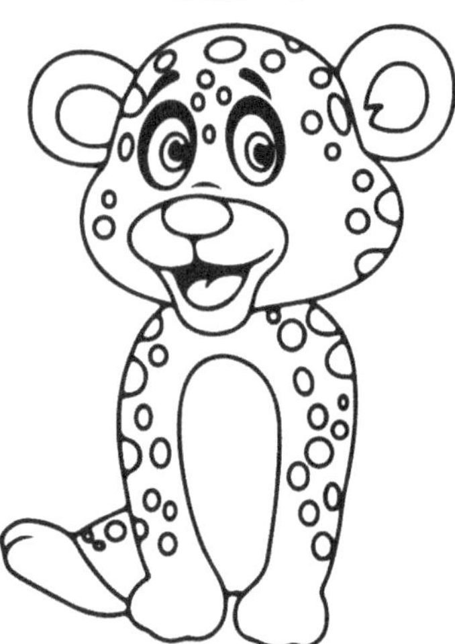

STEP - 6

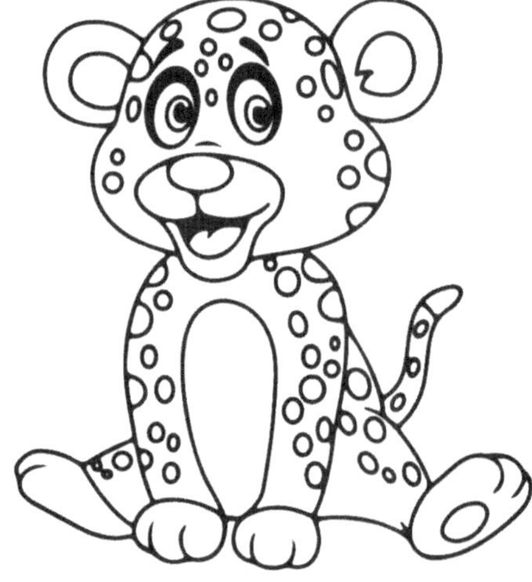

Your Test Pages

STEP - 1

STEP - 2

STEP - 3

STEP - 4

STEP - 5

STEP - 6

HOW TO DRAW

STEP - 1

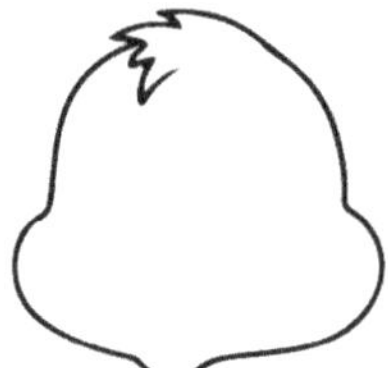

STEP - 2

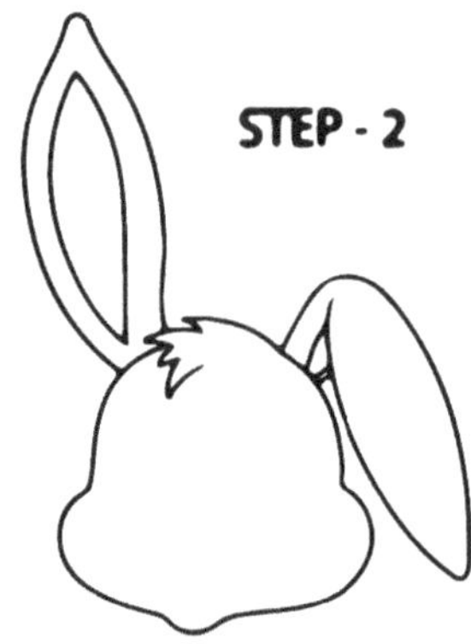

STEP - 3

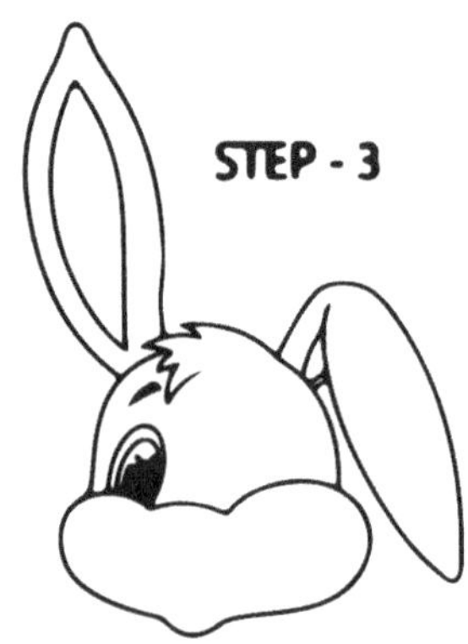

STEP - 4

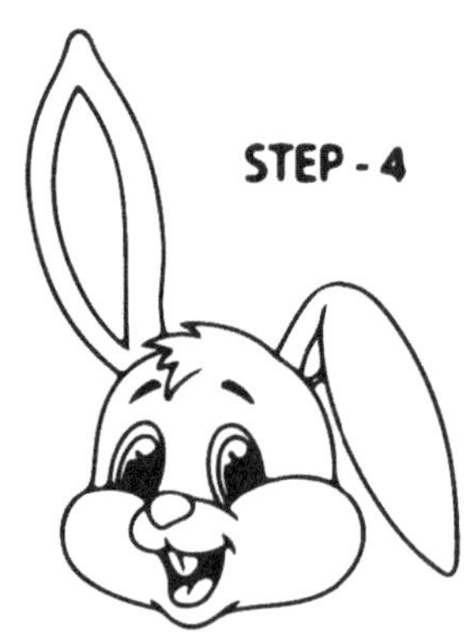

STEP - 5

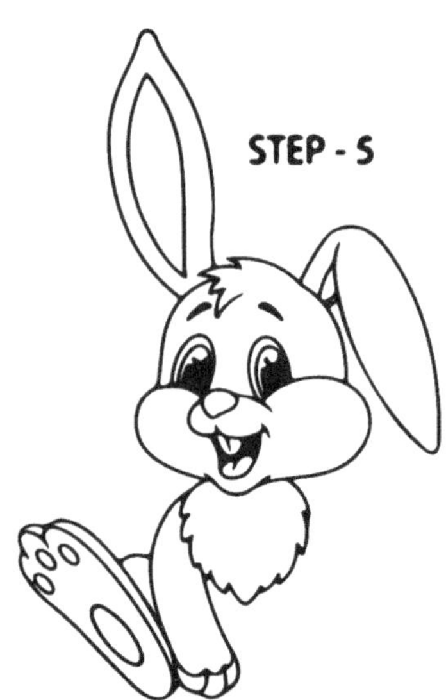

STEP - 6

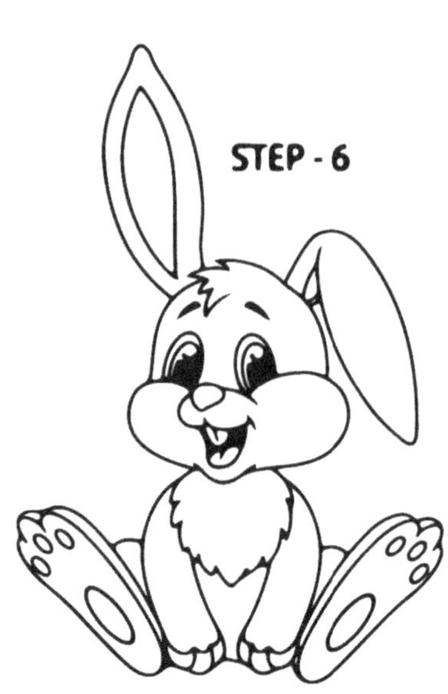

Your Test Pages

STEP - 1

STEP - 2

STEP - 3

STEP - 4

STEP - 5

STEP - 6

HOW TO DRAW

STEP - 1

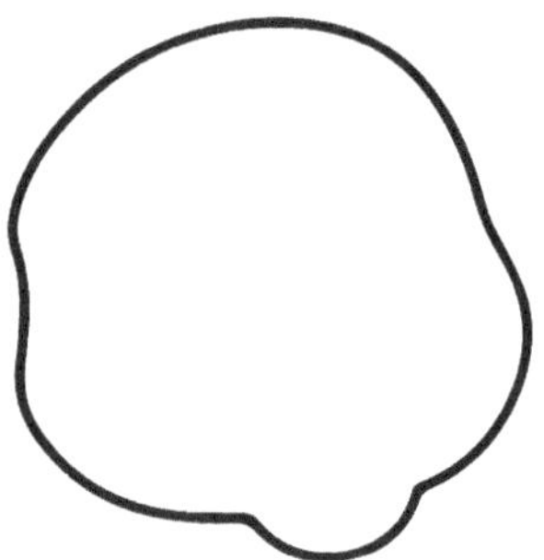

STEP - 2

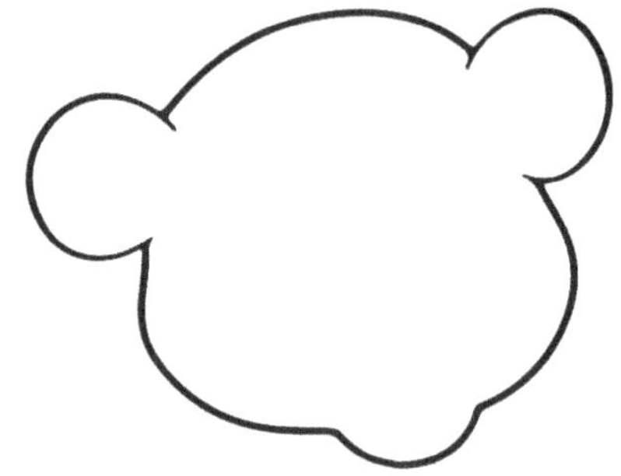

STEP - 3

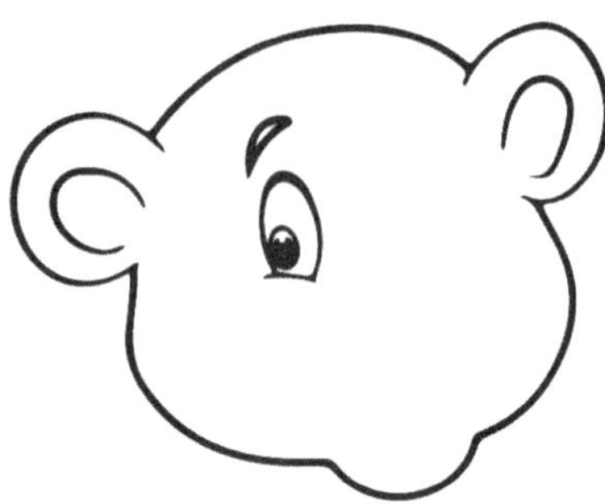

STEP - 4

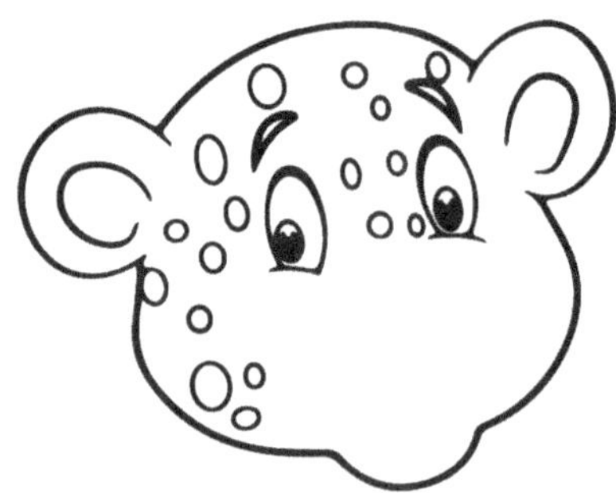

STEP - 5

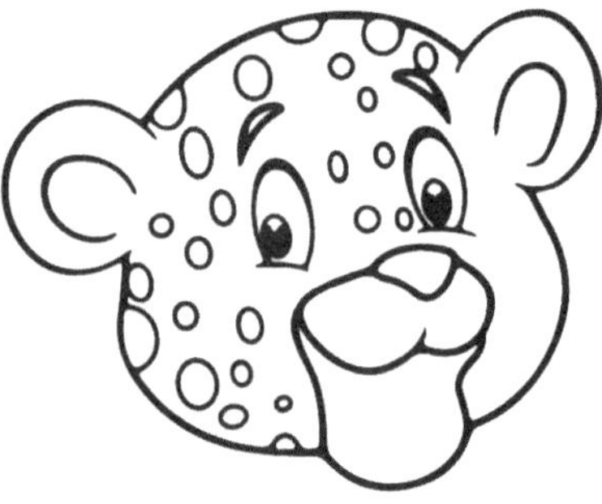

STEP - 6

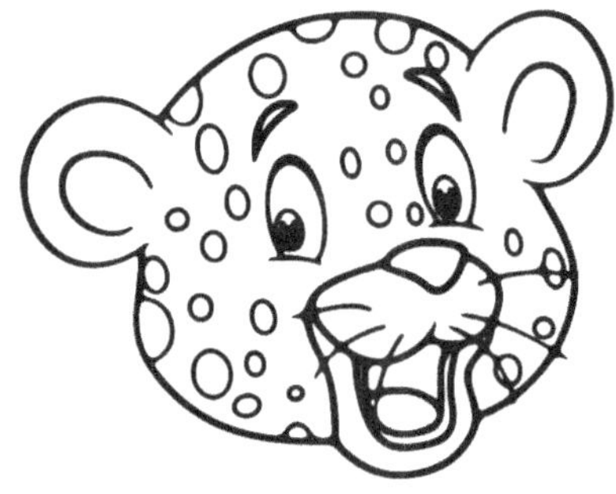

STEP - 1

STEP - 2

STEP - 3

STEP - 4

STEP - 5

STEP - 6

HOW TO DRAW

STEP - 1

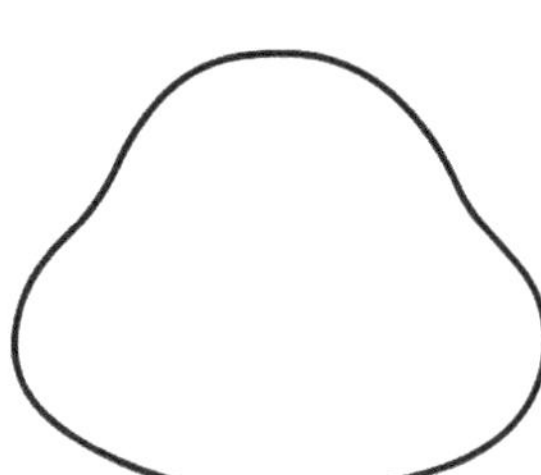

STEP - 2

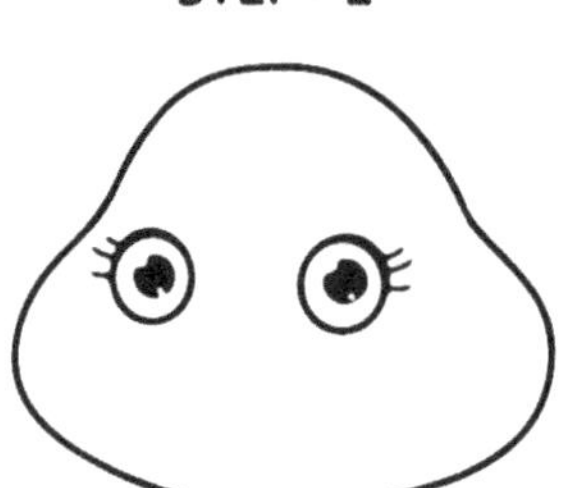

STEP - 3

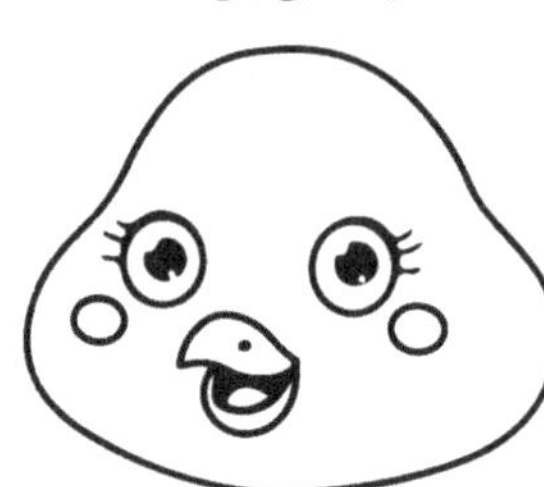

STEP - 4

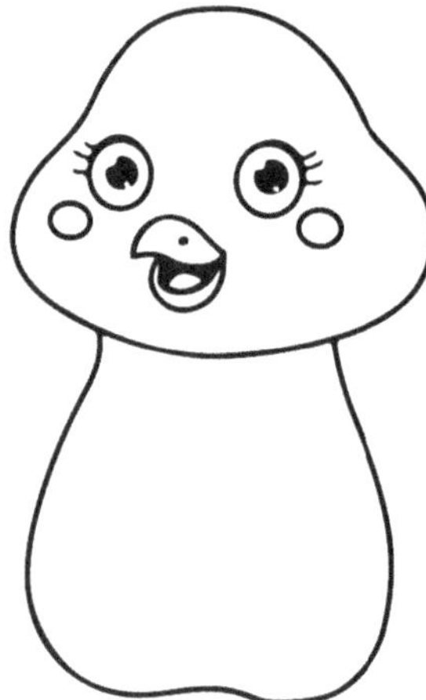

STEP - 5

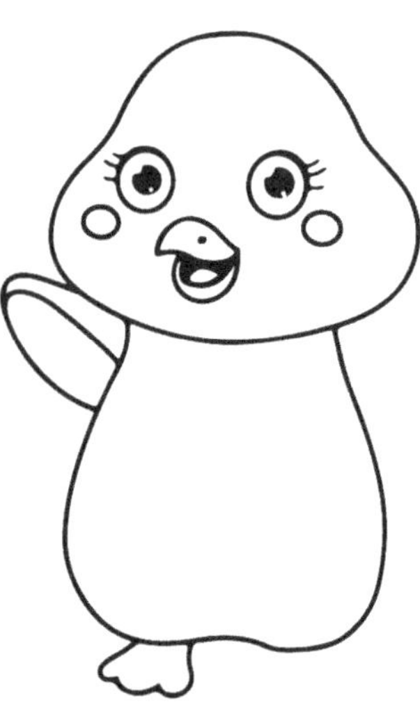

STEP - 6

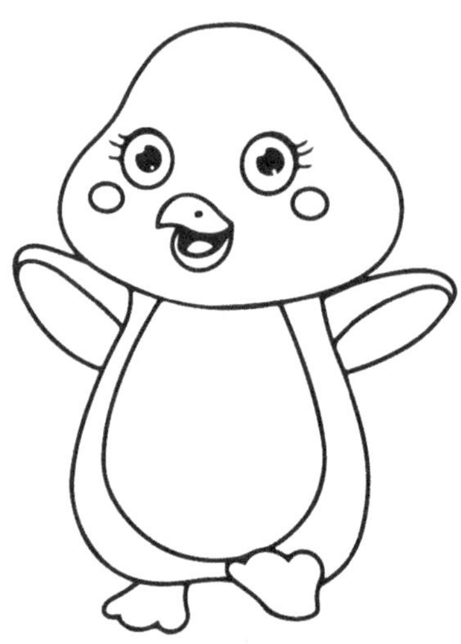

Your Test Pages

STEP - 1

STEP - 2

STEP - 3

STEP - 4

STEP - 5

STEP - 6

HOW TO DRAW

STEP - 1
STEP - 2

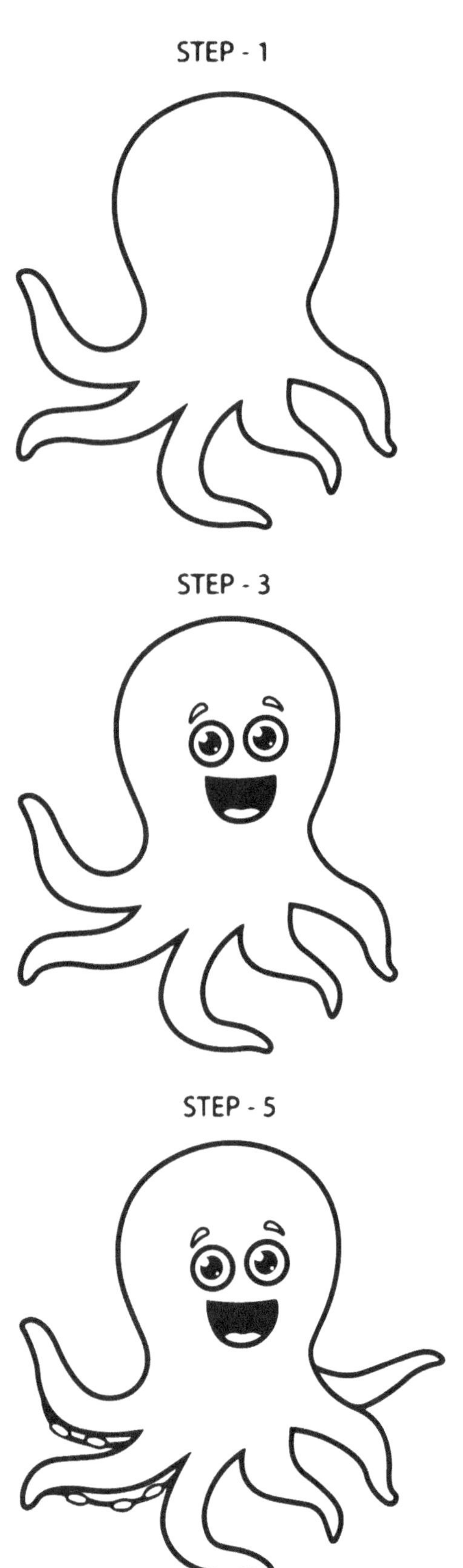

STEP - 3
STEP - 4

STEP - 5
STEP - 6

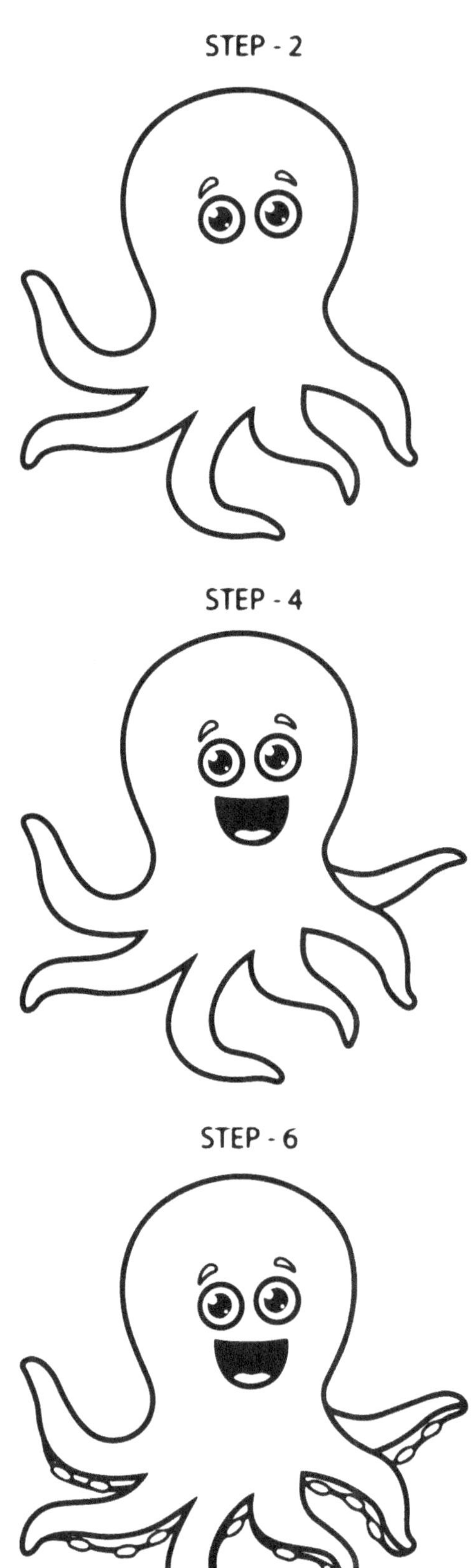

STEP - 1

STEP - 2

STEP - 3

STEP - 4

STEP - 5

STEP - 6

HOW TO DRAW

STEP - 1

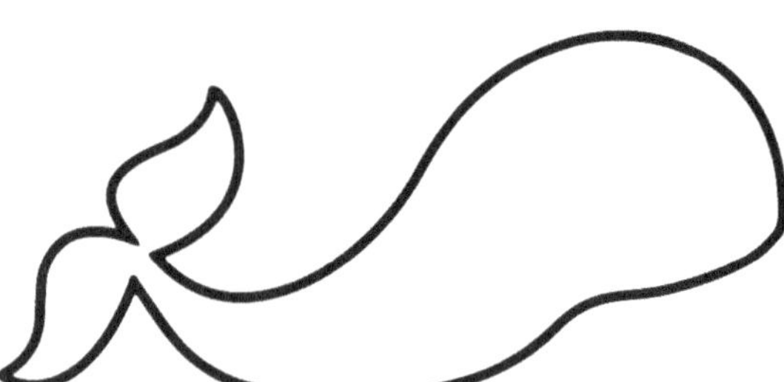

STEP - 2

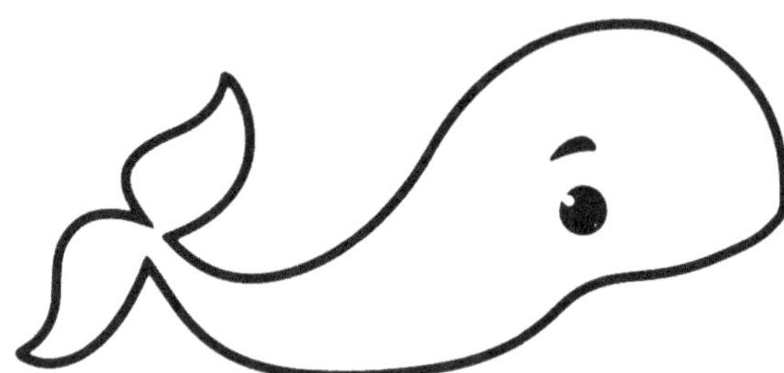

STEP - 3

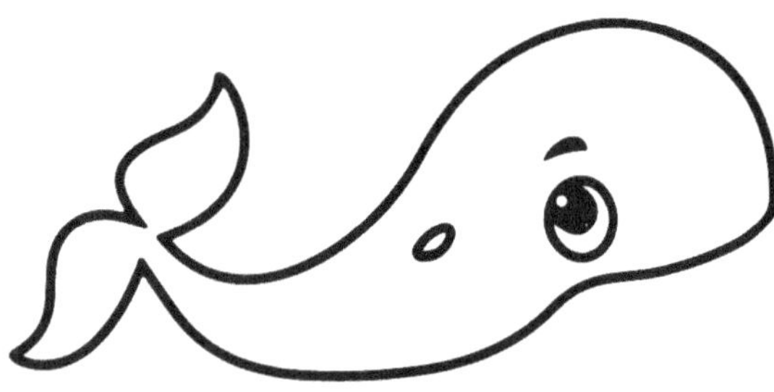

STEP - 4

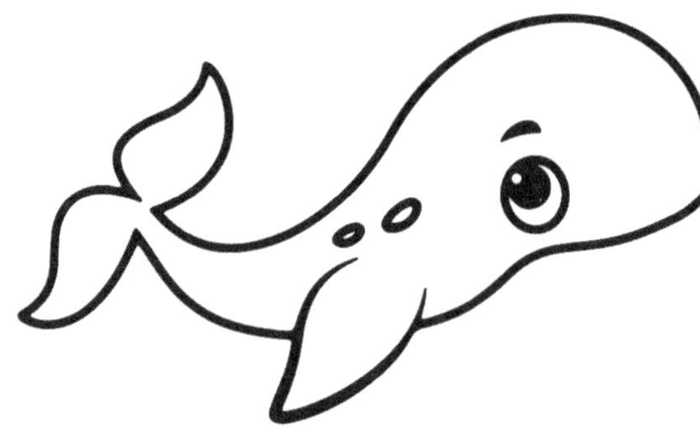

STEP - 5

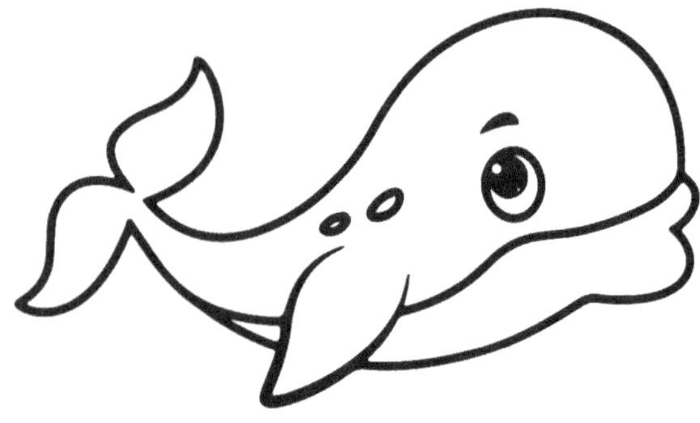

STEP - 6

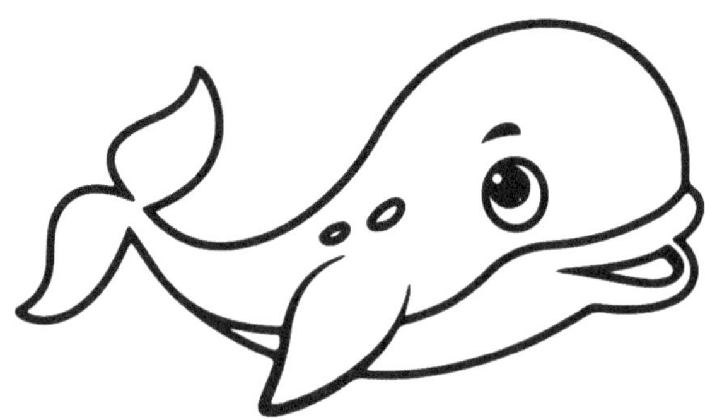

Your Test Pages

STEP - 1

STEP - 2

STEP - 3

STEP - 4

STEP - 5

STEP - 6

HOW TO DRAW

STEP - 1

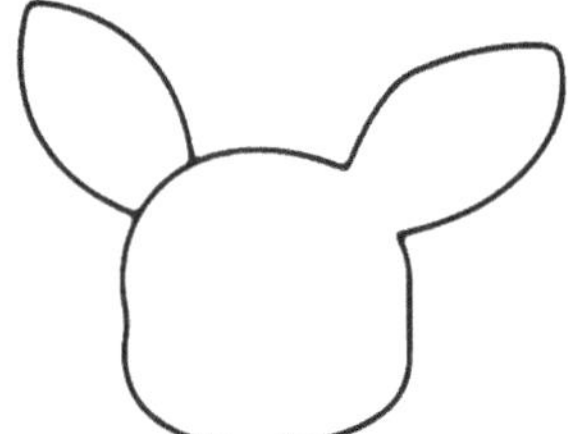

STEP - 2

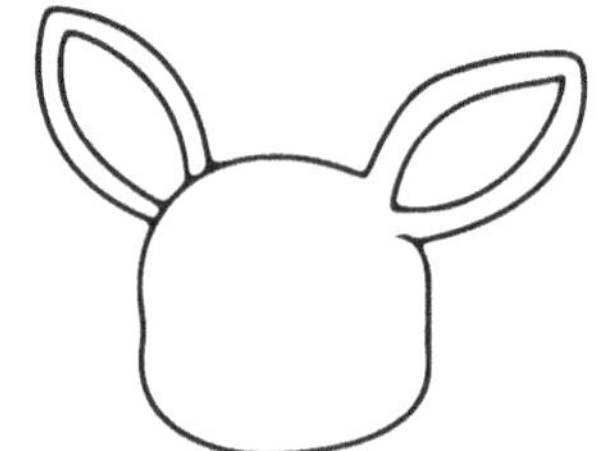

STEP - 3

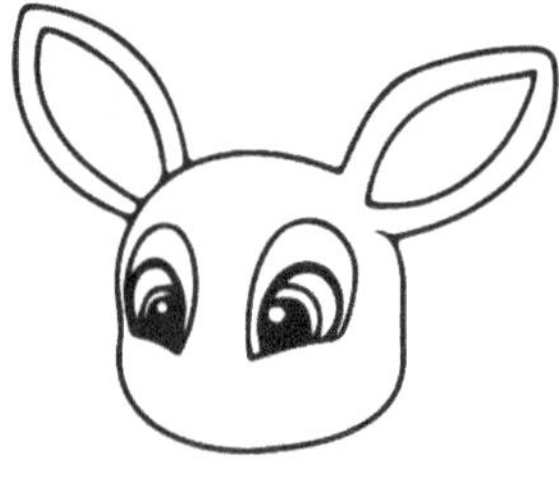

STEP - 4

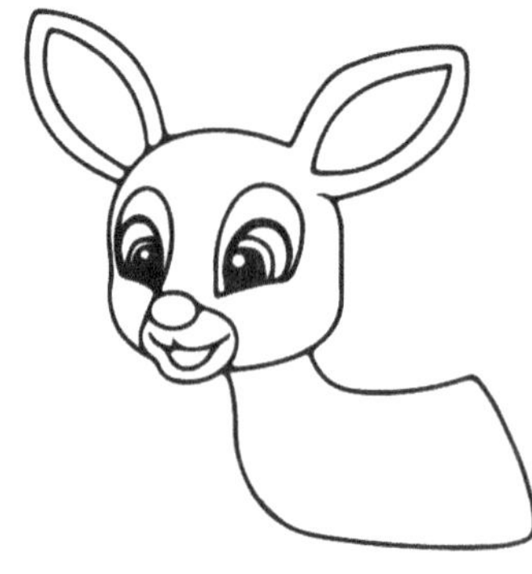

STEP - 5

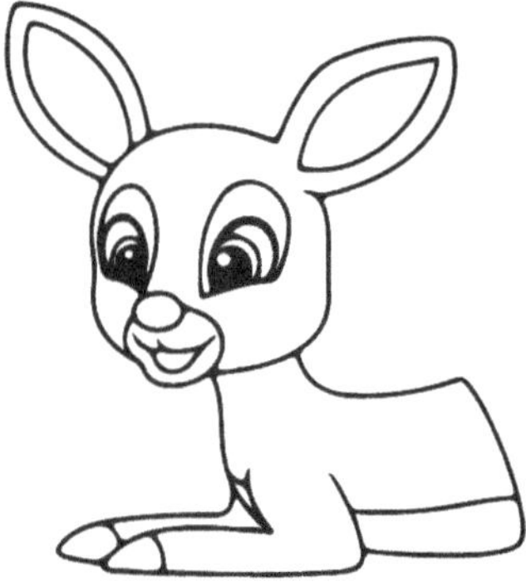

STEP - 6

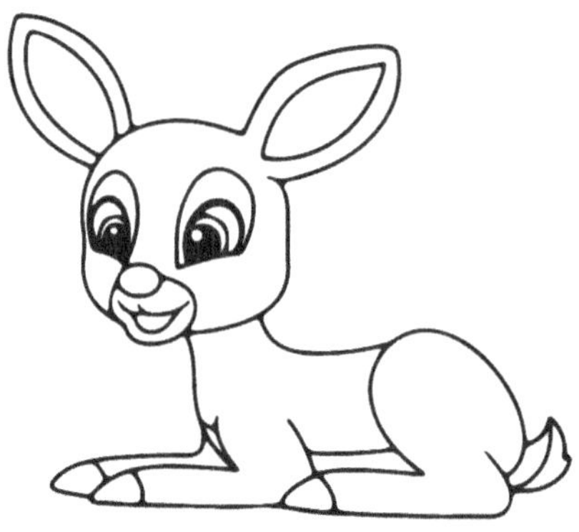

Your Test Pages

STEP - 1

STEP - 2

STEP - 3

STEP - 4

STEP - 5

STEP - 6

HOW TO DRAW

STEP - 1

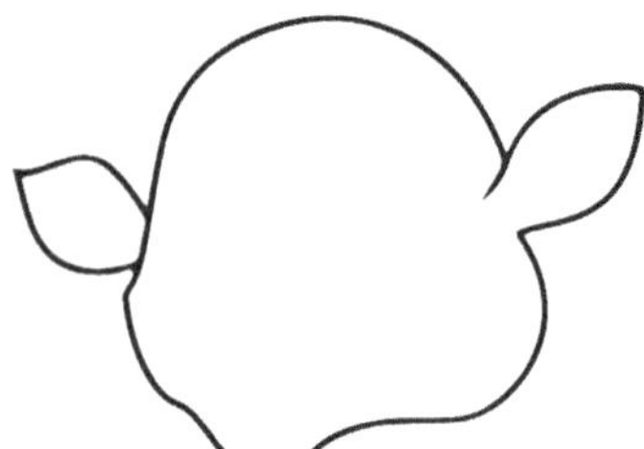

STEP - 2

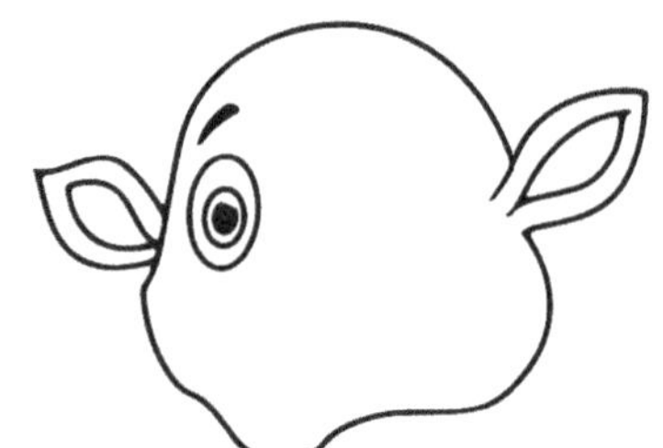

STEP - 3

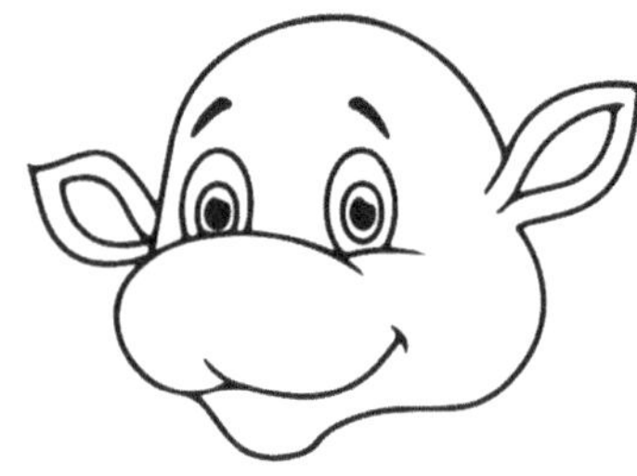

STEP - 4

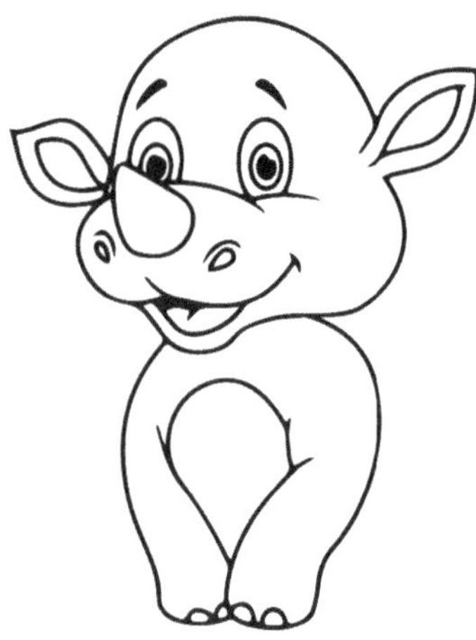

STEP - 5

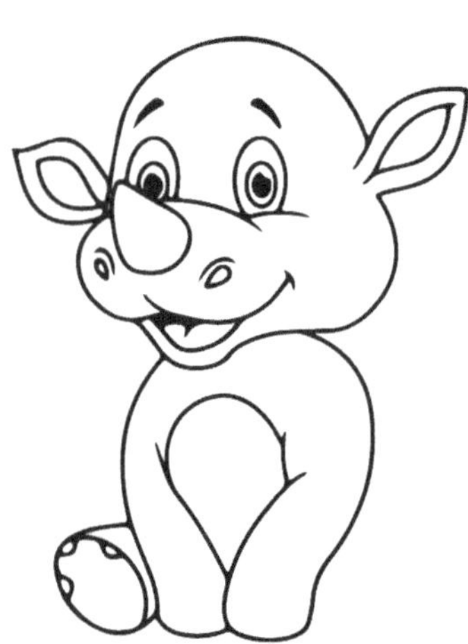

STEP - 6

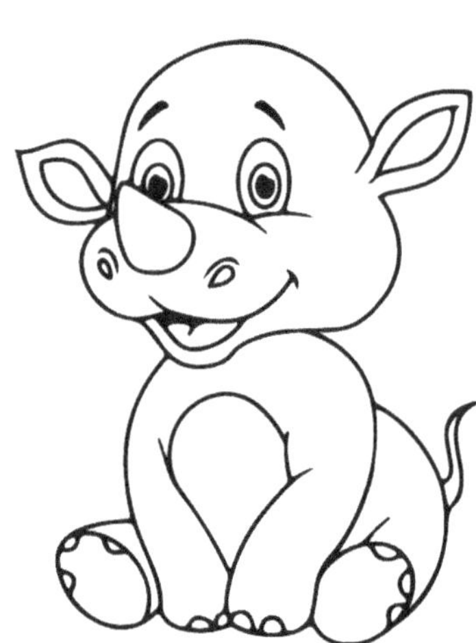

Your Test Pages

STEP - 1

STEP - 2

STEP - 3

STEP - 4

STEP - 5

STEP - 6

HOW TO DRAW

STEP - 1

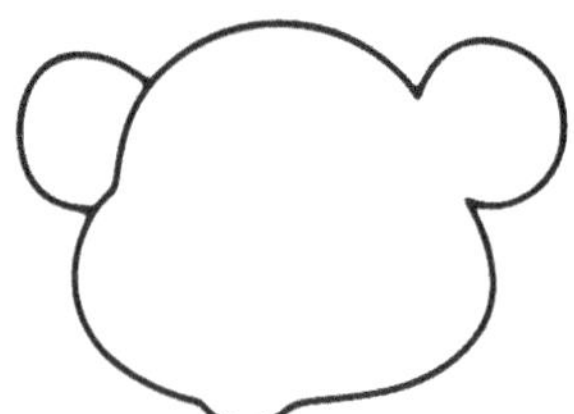

STEP - 2

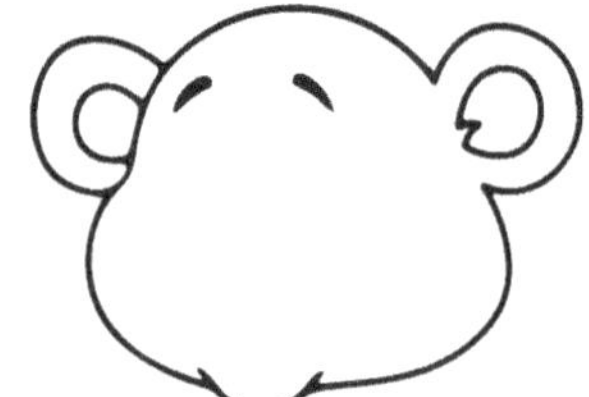

STEP - 3

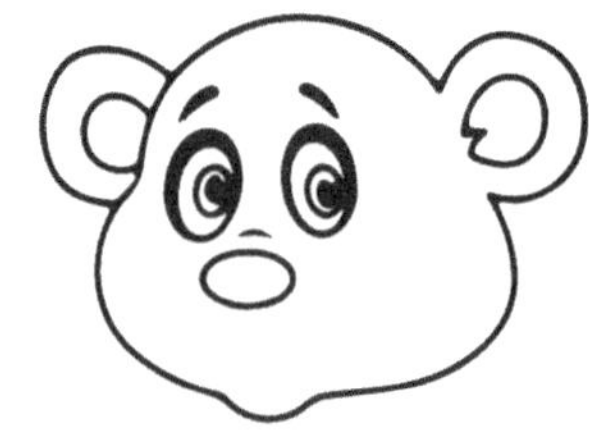

STEP - 4

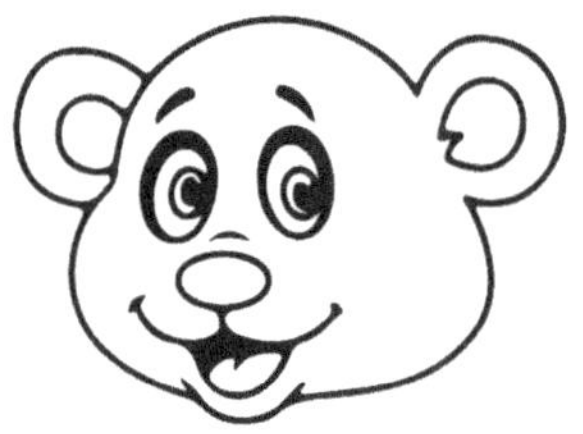

STEP - 5

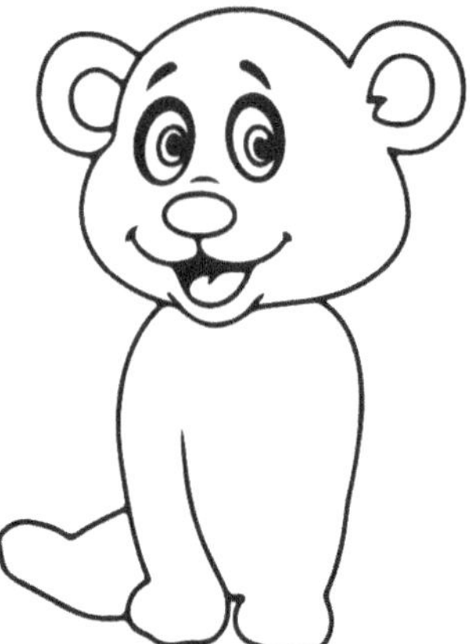

STEP - 6

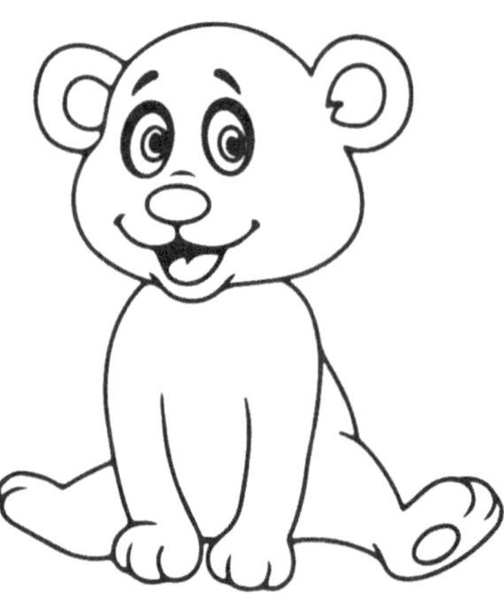

Your Test Pages

STEP - 1

STEP - 2

STEP - 3

STEP - 4

STEP - 5

STEP - 6

HOW TO DRAW

STEP - 1

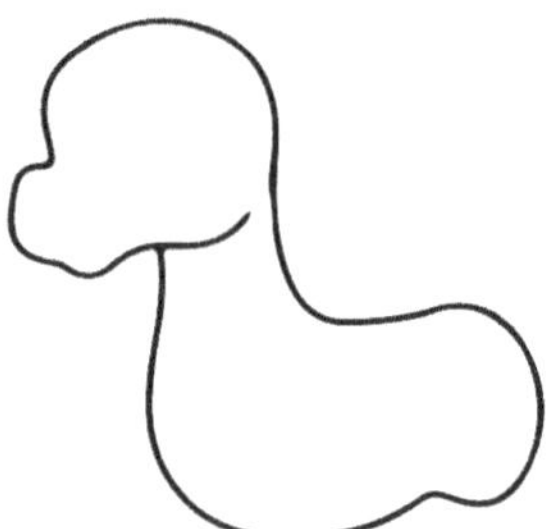

STEP - 2

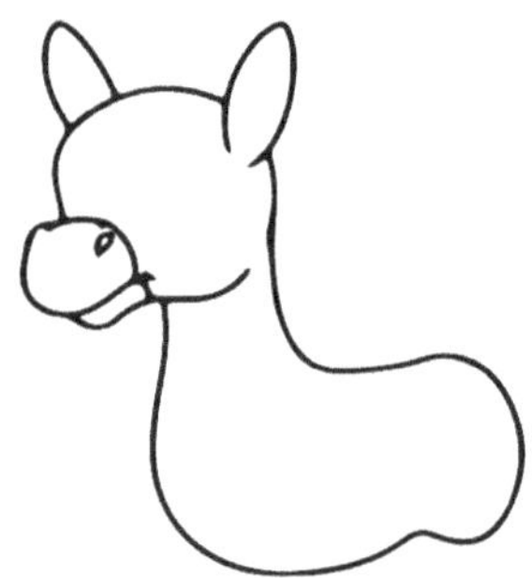

STEP - 3

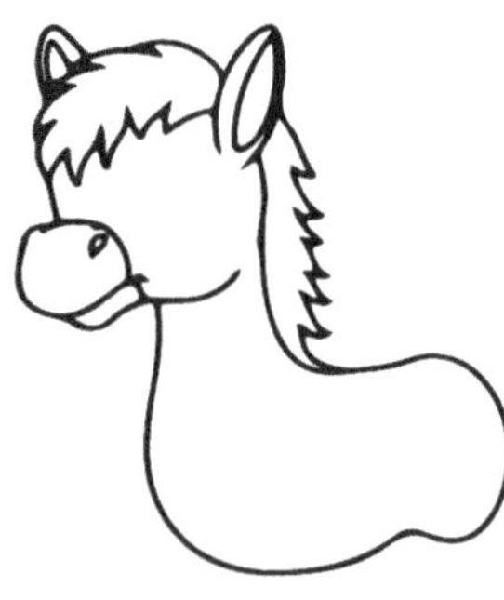

STEP - 4

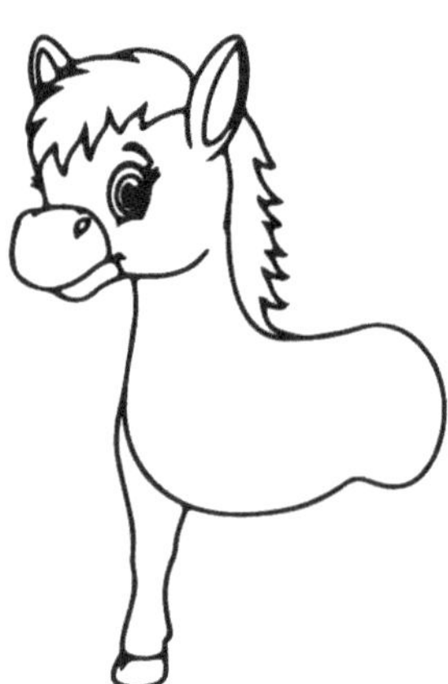

STEP - 5

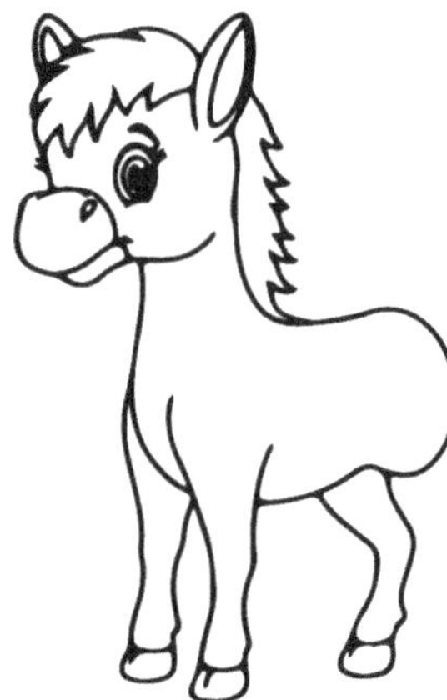

STEP - 6

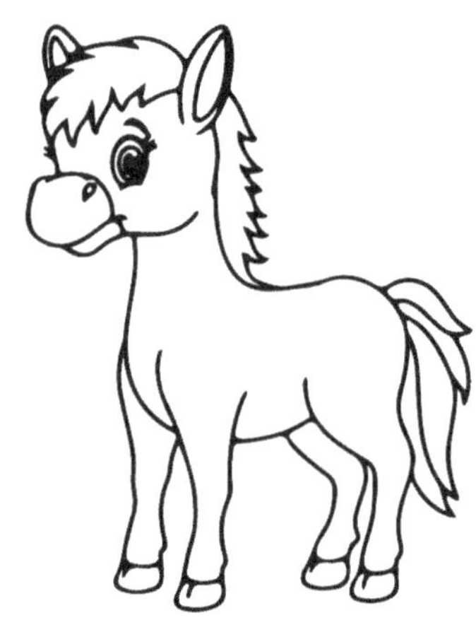

Your Test Pages

STEP - 1

STEP - 2

STEP - 3

STEP - 4

STEP - 5

STEP - 6

HOW TO DRAW

STEP - 1

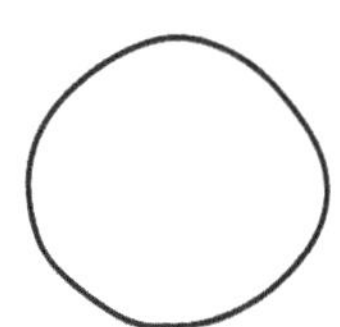

STEP - 2

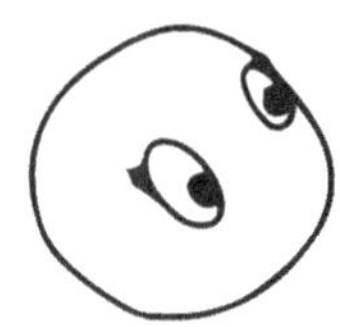

STEP - 3

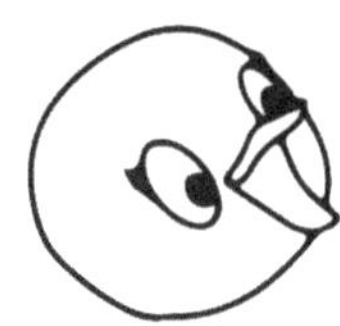

STEP - 4

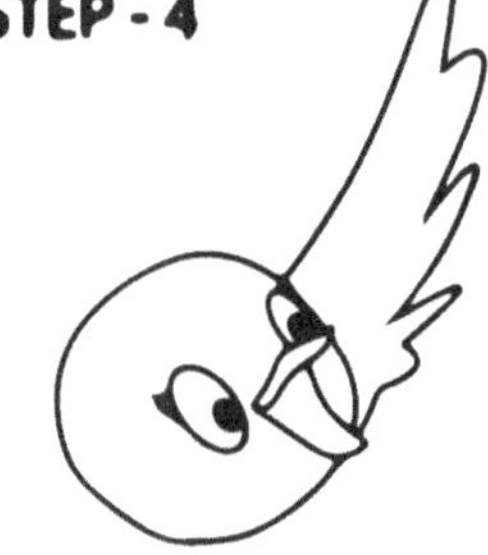

STEP - 5

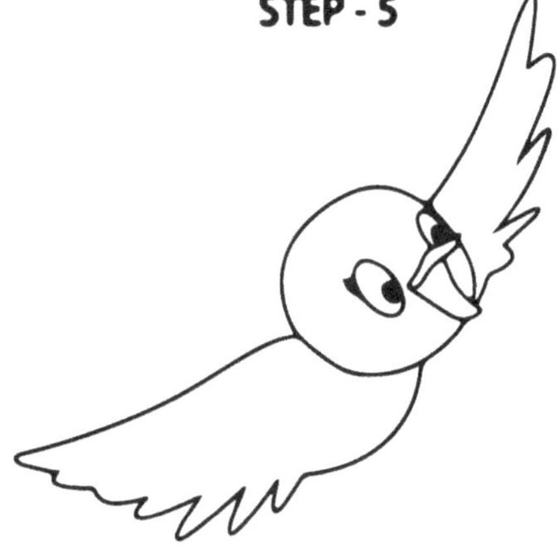

STEP - 6

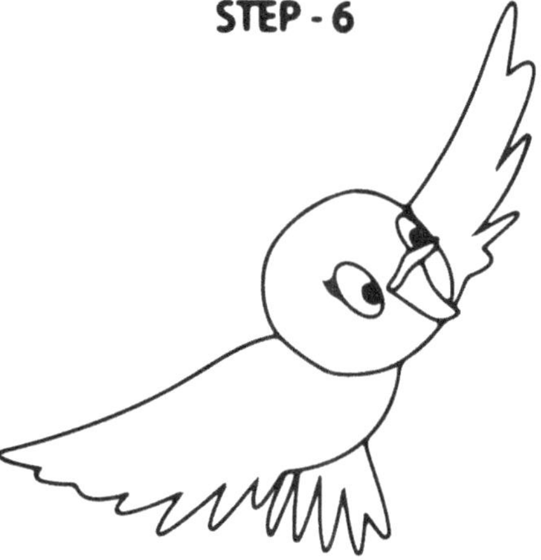

Your Test Pages

STEP - 1

STEP - 2

STEP - 3

STEP - 4

STEP - 5

STEP - 6

HOW TO DRAW

STEP - 1

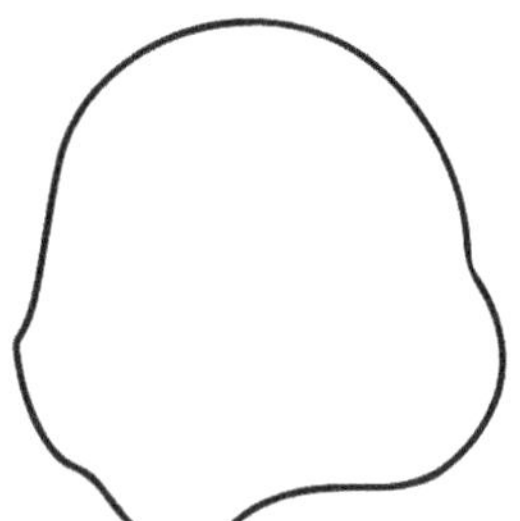

STEP - 2

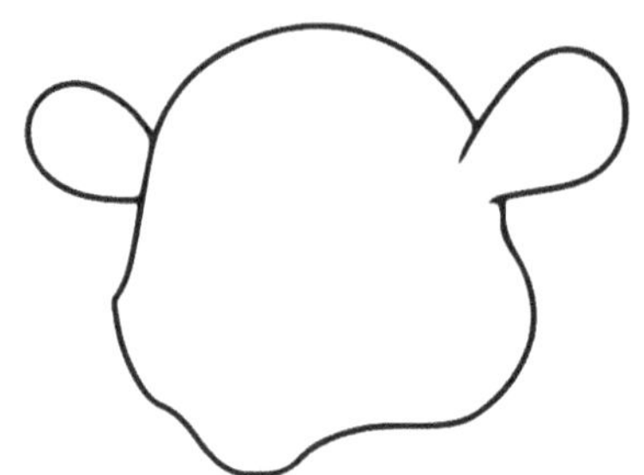

STEP - 3

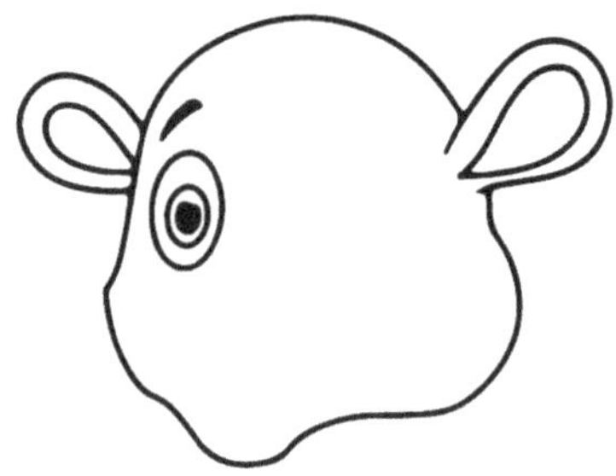

STEP - 4

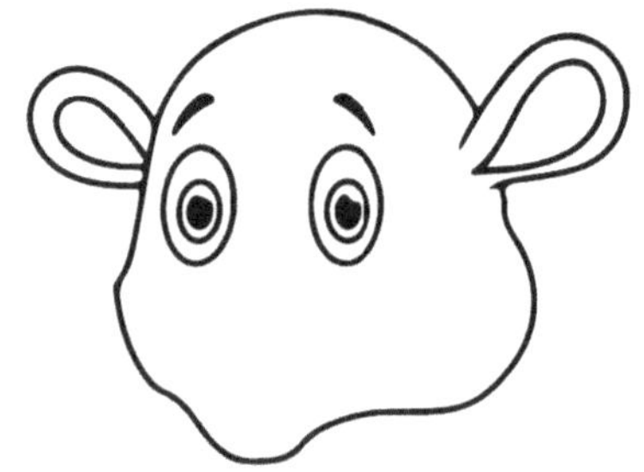

STEP - 5

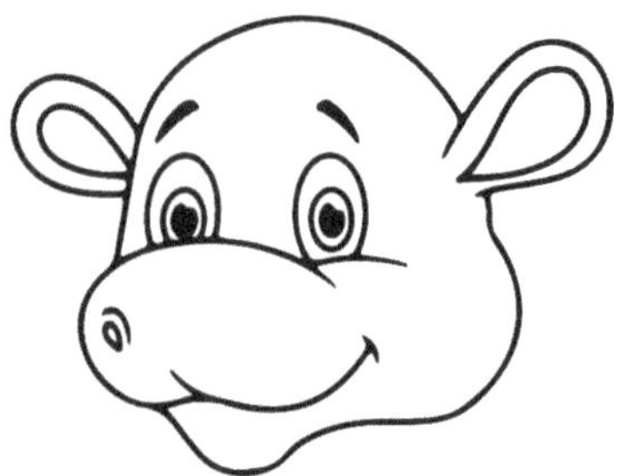

STEP - 6

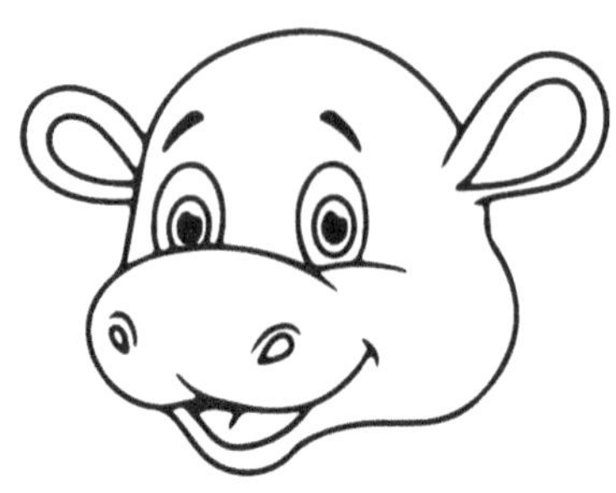

Your Test Pages

STEP - 1

STEP - 2

STEP - 3

STEP - 4

STEP - 5

STEP - 6

HOW TO DRAW

STEP - 1

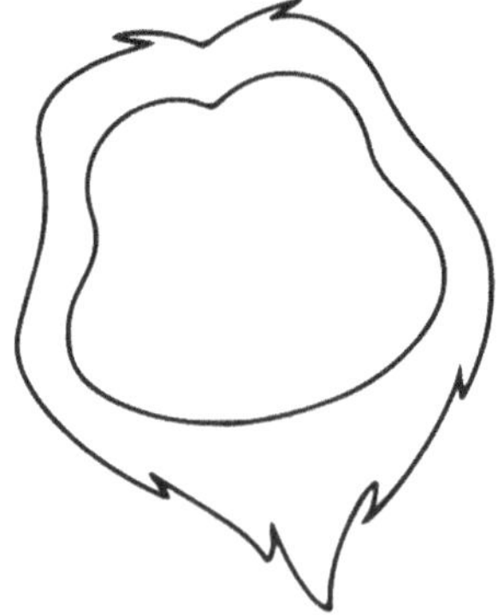

STEP - 2

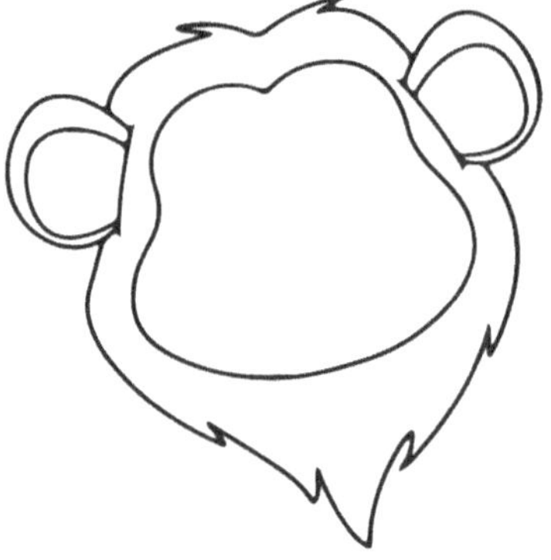

STEP - 3

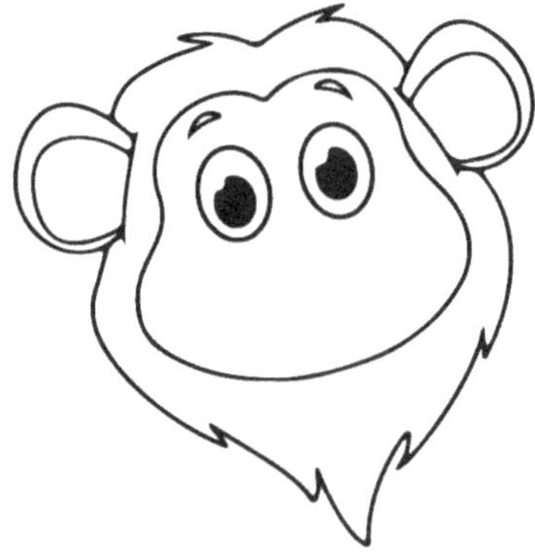

STEP - 4

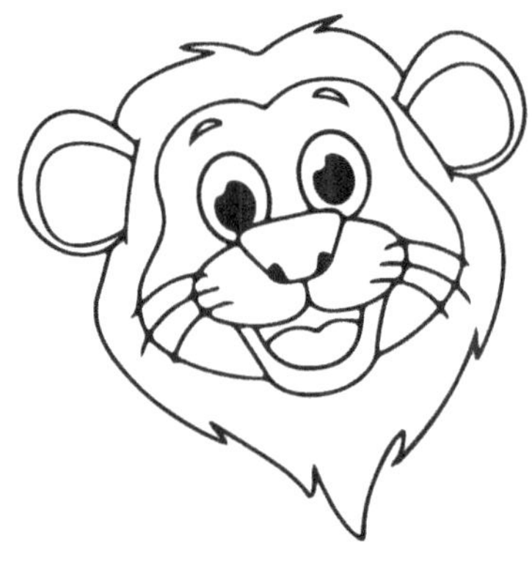

STEP - 5

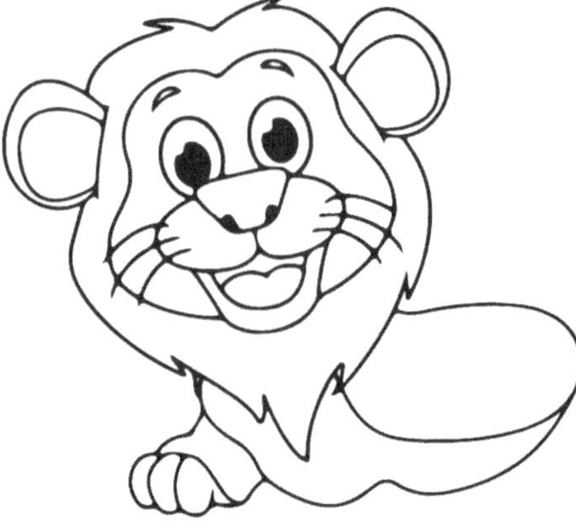

STEP - 6

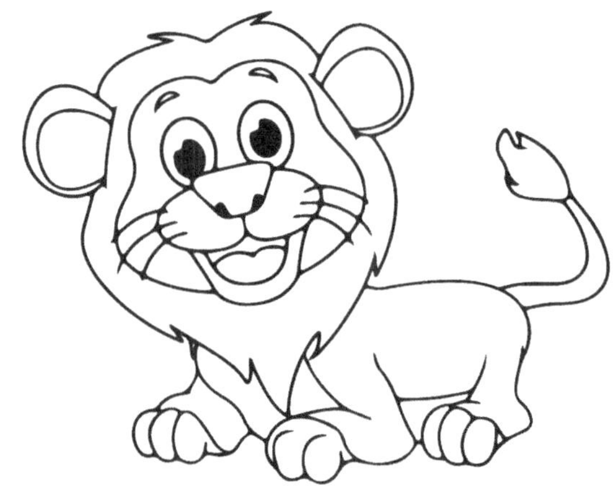

Your Test Pages

STEP - 1

STEP - 2

STEP - 3

STEP - 4

STEP - 5

STEP - 6

HOW TO DRAW

STEP - 1
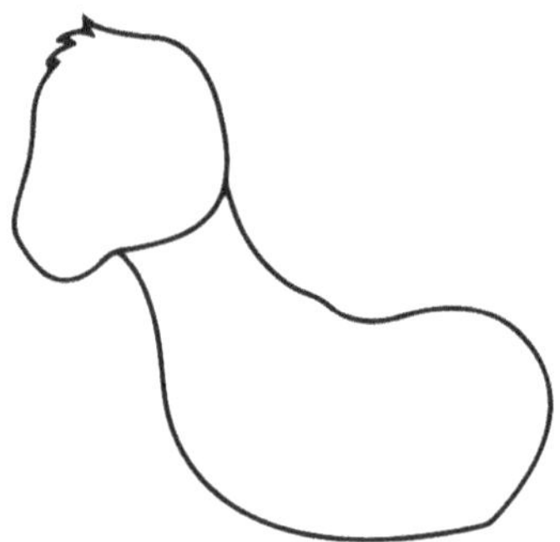

STEP - 2
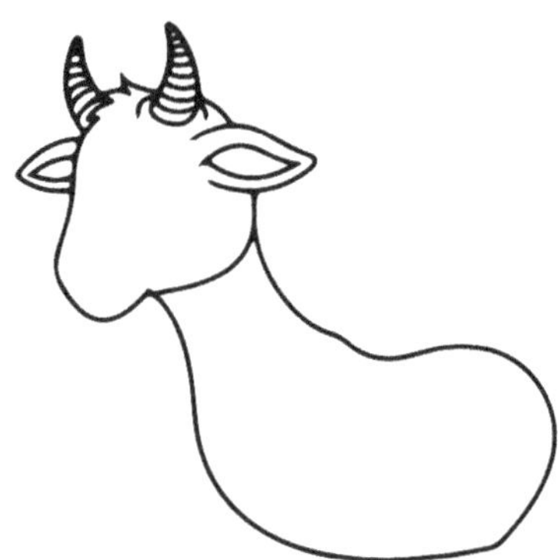

STEP - 3
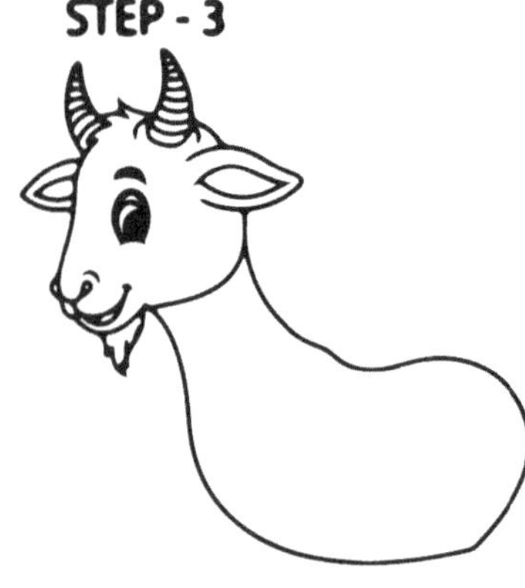

STEP - 4
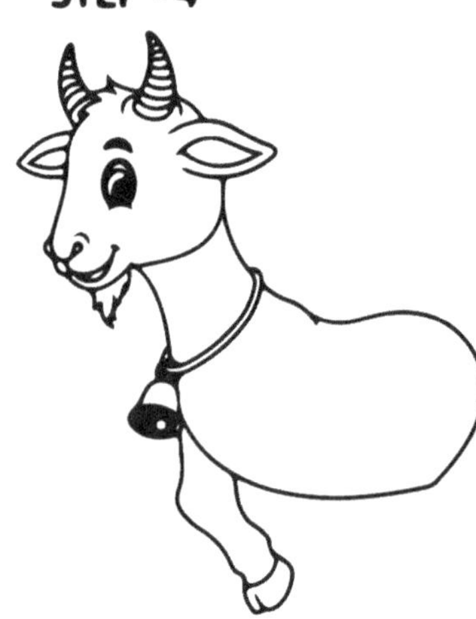

STEP - 5
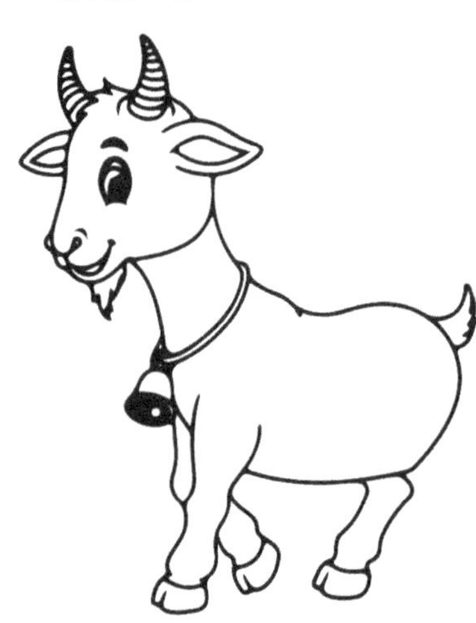

STEP - 6
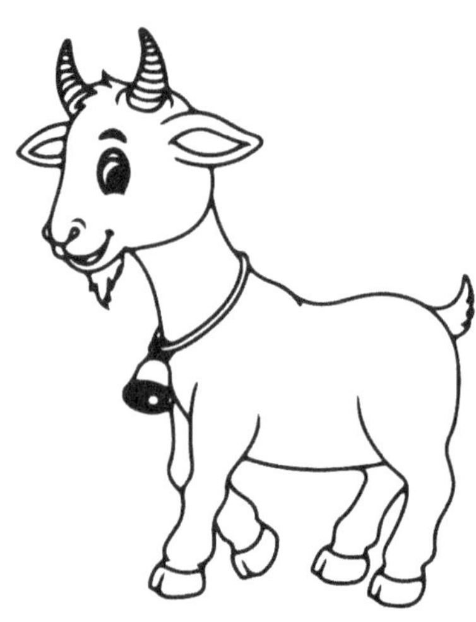

Your Test Pages

STEP - 1

STEP - 2

STEP - 3

STEP - 4

STEP - 5

STEP - 6

HOW TO DRAW

STEP - 1
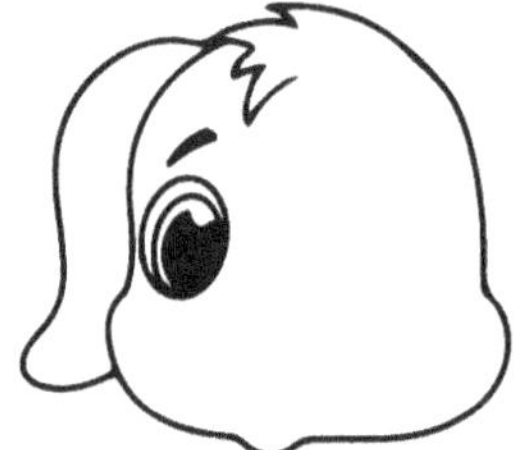

STEP - 2
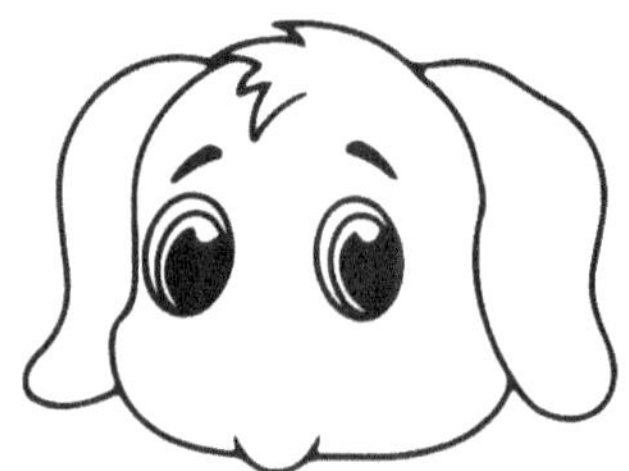

STEP - 3
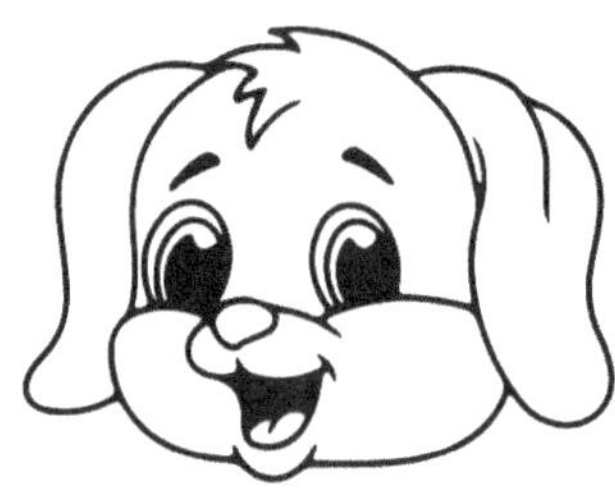

STEP - 4
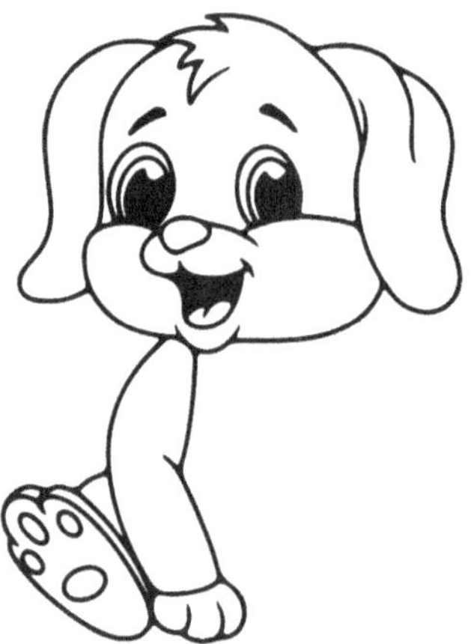

STEP - 5
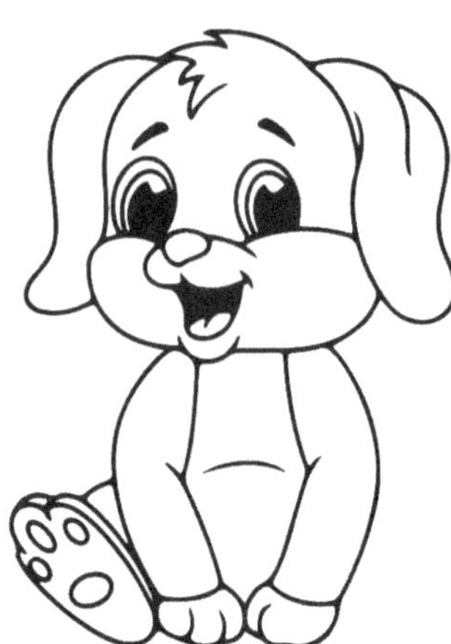

STEP - 6
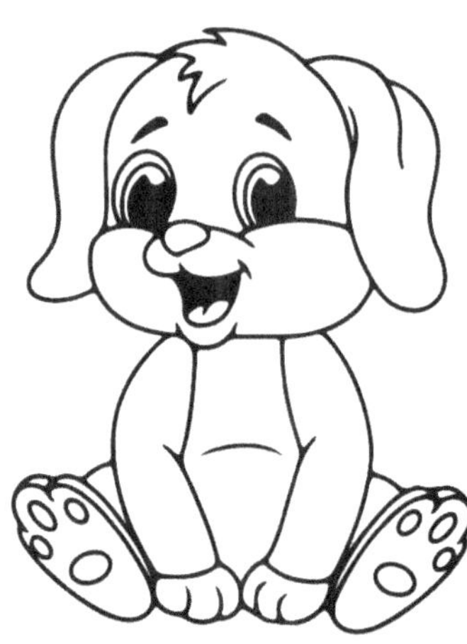

Your Test Pages

STEP - 1

STEP - 2

STEP - 3

STEP - 4

STEP - 5

STEP - 6

HOW TO DRAW

STEP - 1

STEP - 2

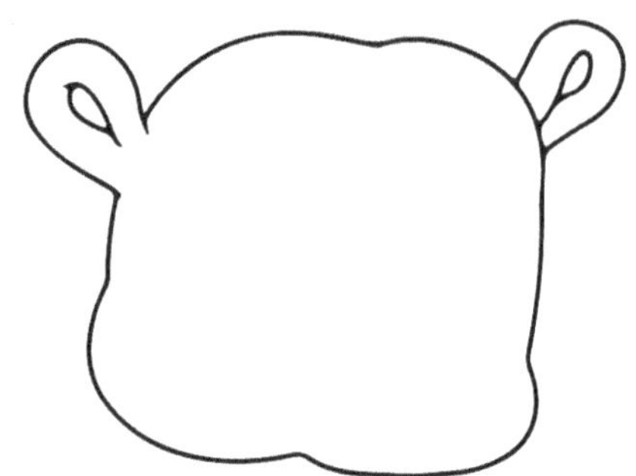

STEP - 3

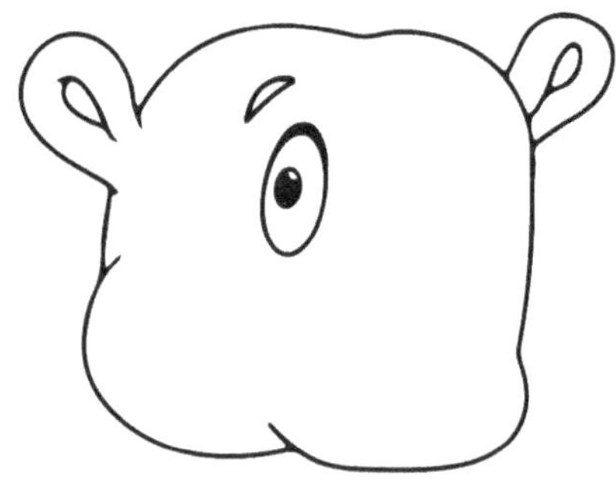

STEP - 4

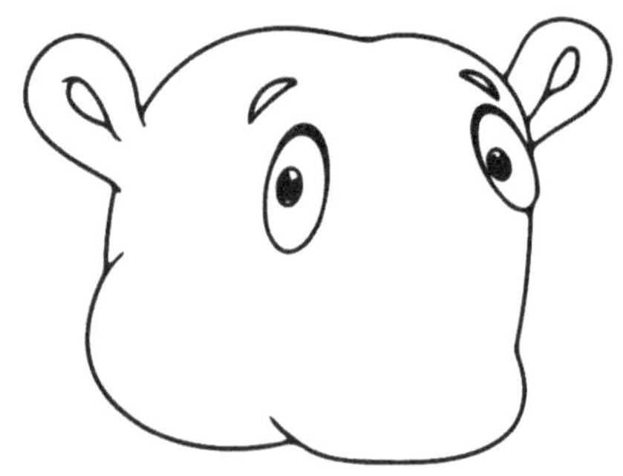

STEP - 5

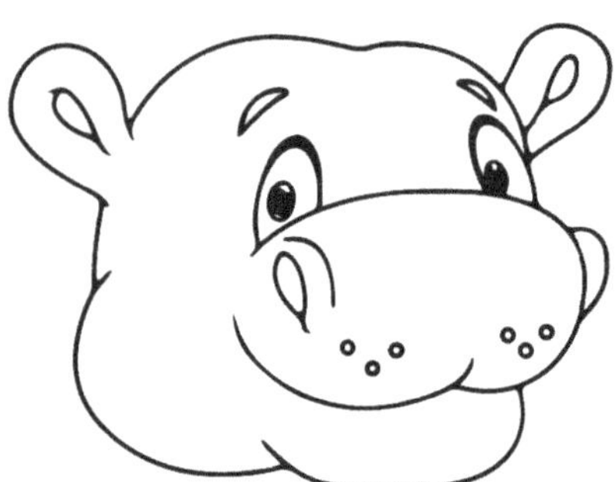

STEP - 6

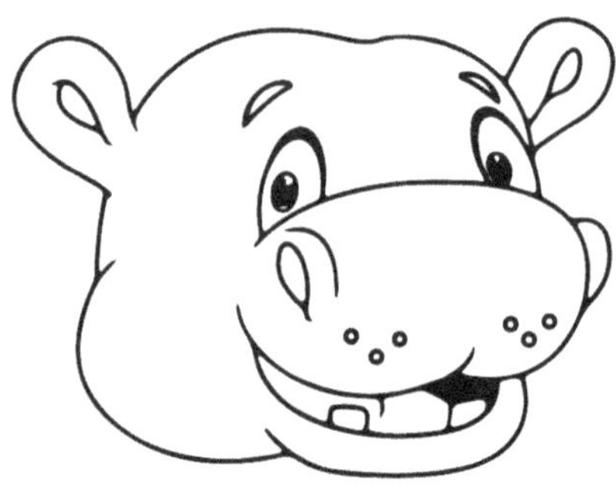

Your Test Pages

STEP - 1

STEP - 2

STEP - 3

STEP - 4

STEP - 5

STEP - 6

HOW TO DRAW

STEP - 1

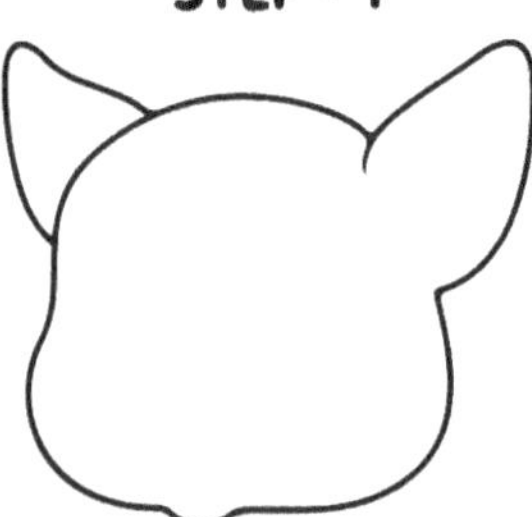

STEP - 2

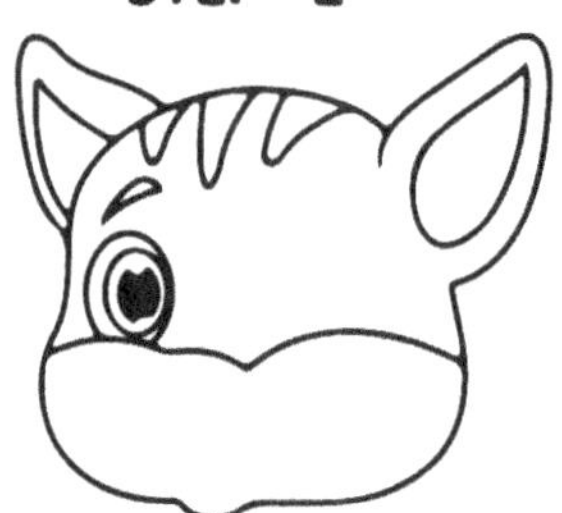

STEP - 3

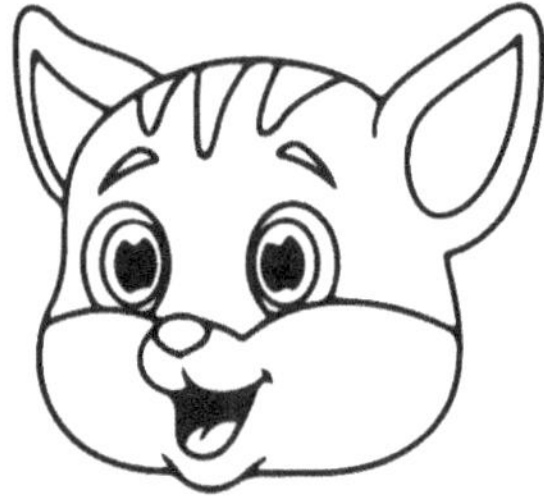

STEP - 4

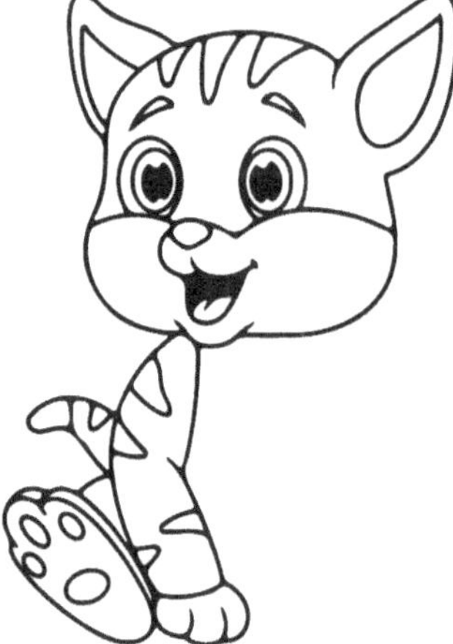

STEP - 5

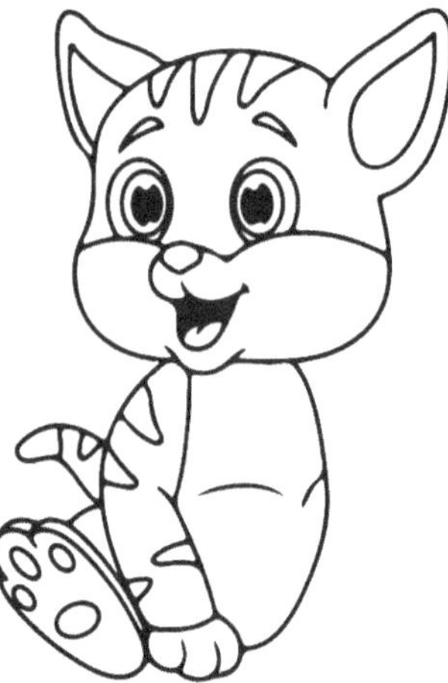

STEP - 6

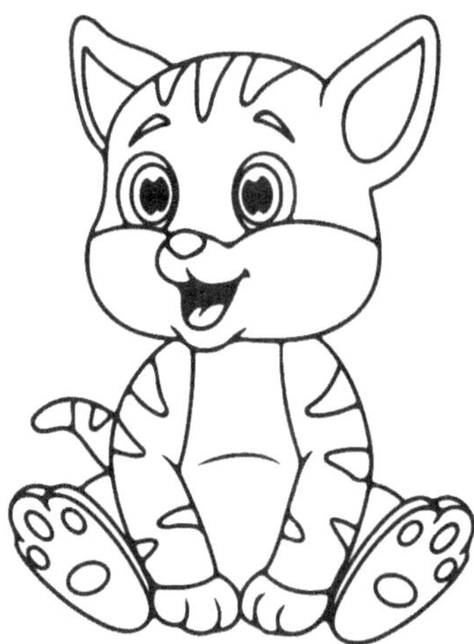

Your Test Pages

STEP - 1

STEP - 2

STEP - 3

STEP - 4

STEP - 5

STEP - 6

HOW TO DRAW

STEP - 1
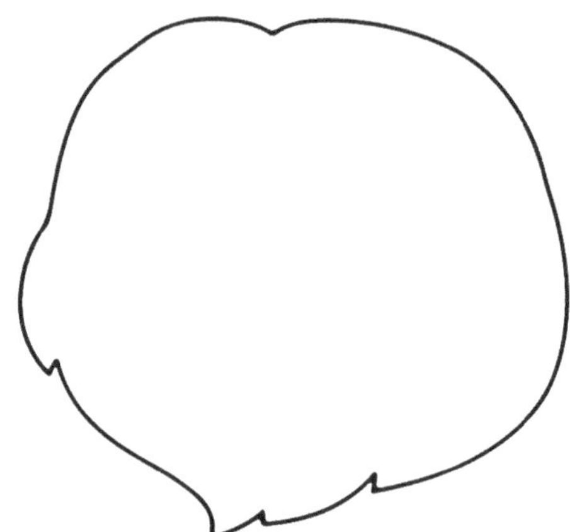

STEP - 2
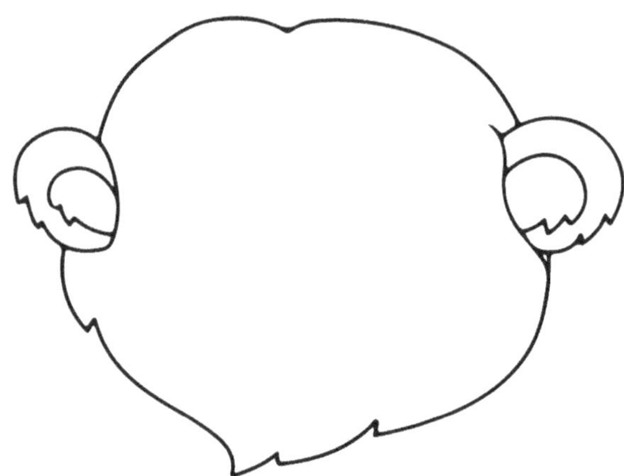

STEP - 3
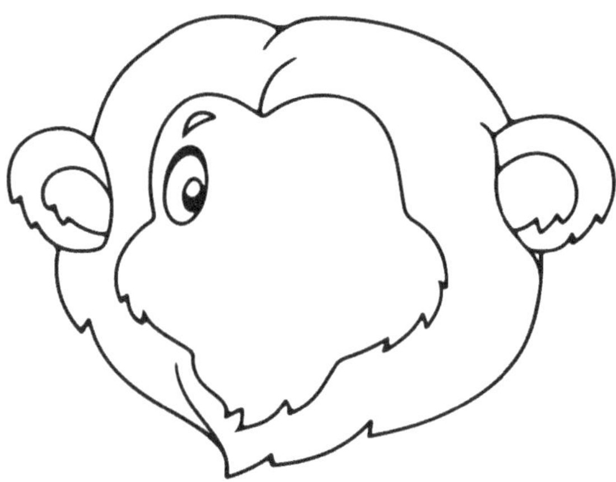

STEP - 4
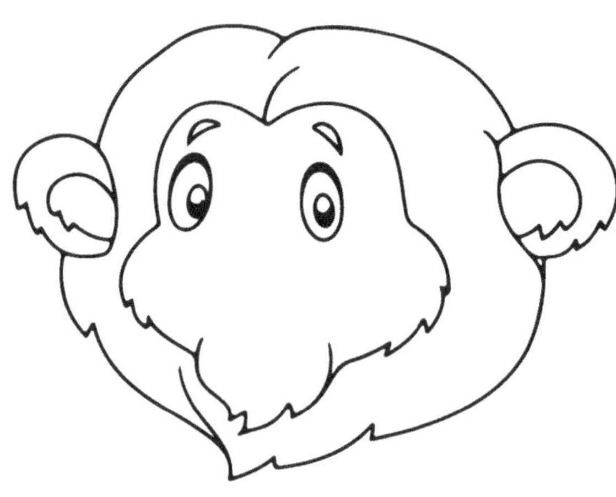

STEP - 5
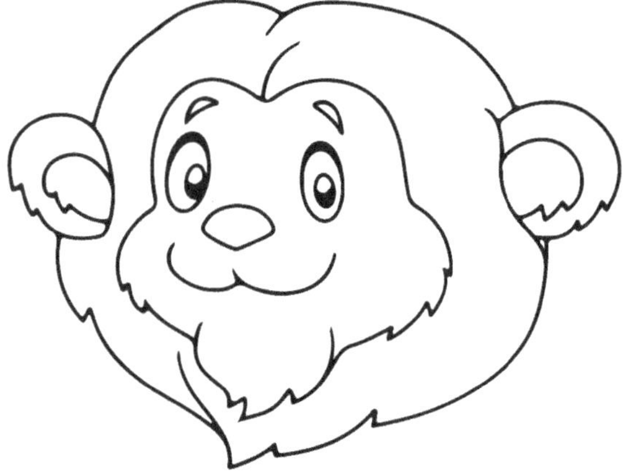

STEP - 6
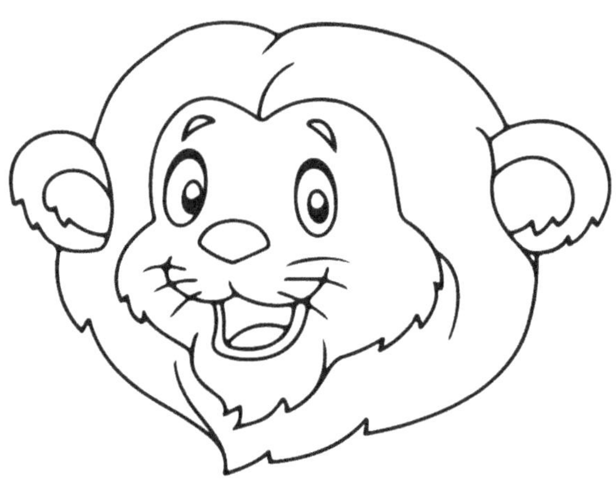

Your Test Pages

STEP - 1

STEP - 2

STEP - 3

STEP - 4

STEP - 5

STEP - 6

HOW TO DRAW

STEP - 1

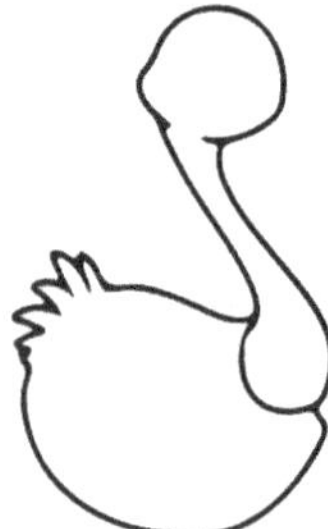

STEP - 2

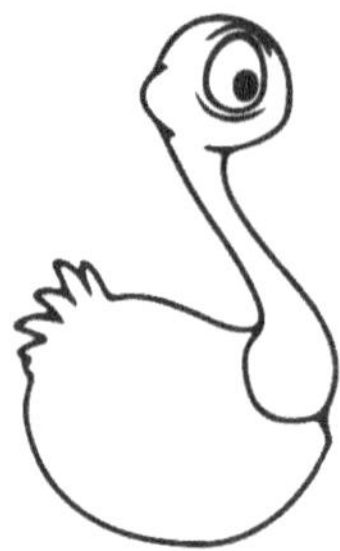

STEP - 3

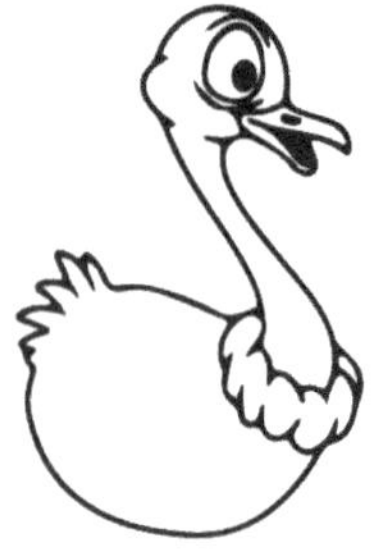

STEP - 4

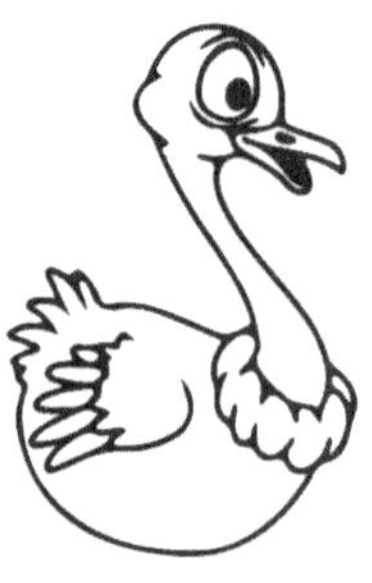

STEP - 5

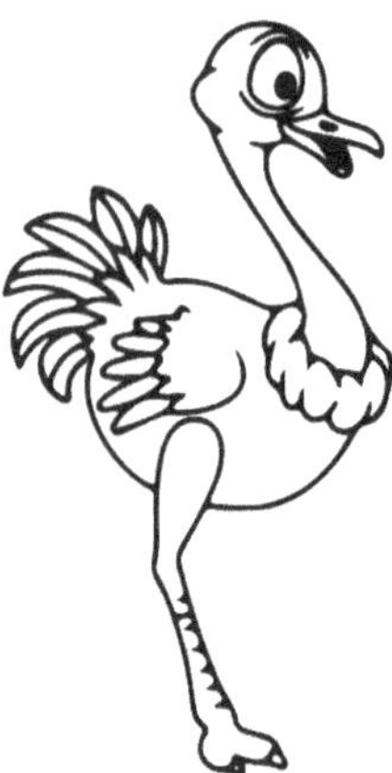

STEP - 6

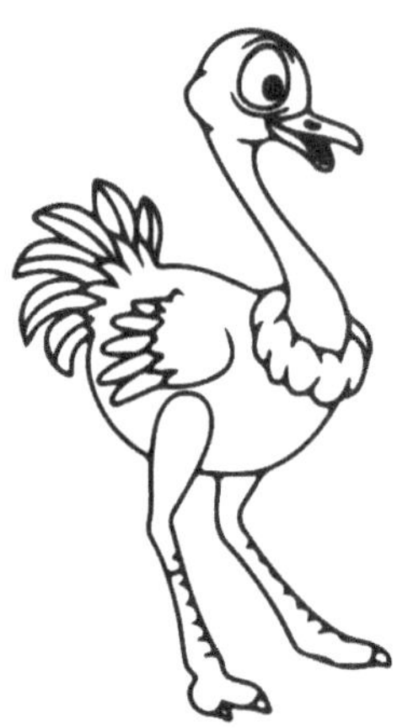

Your Test Pages

STEP - 1

STEP - 2

STEP - 3

STEP - 4

STEP - 5

STEP - 6

HOW TO DRAW

STEP - 1

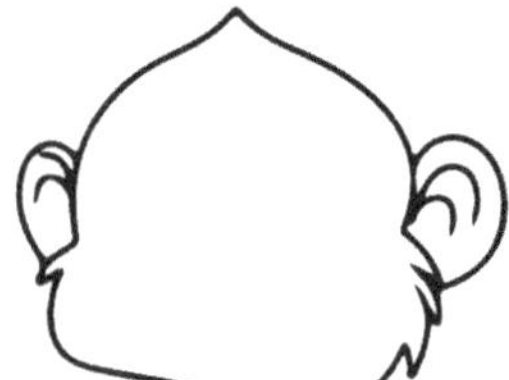

STEP - 2

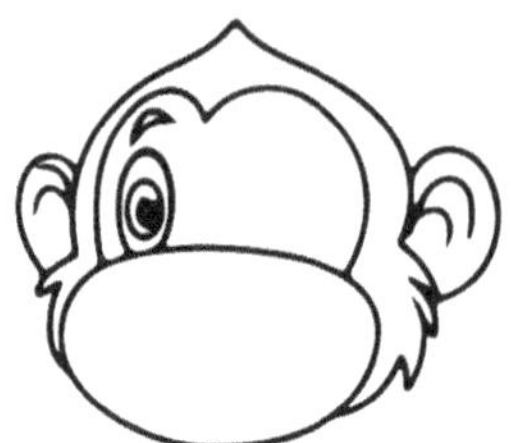

STEP - 3

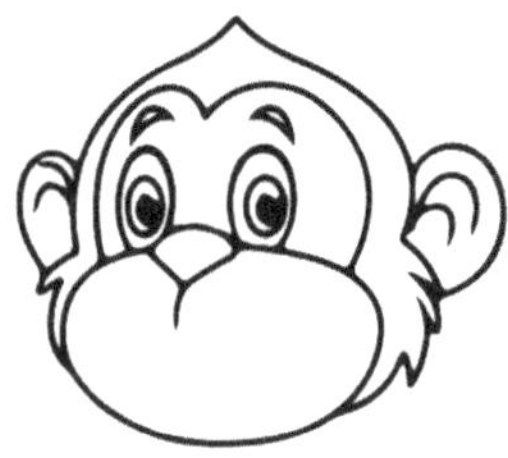

STEP - 4

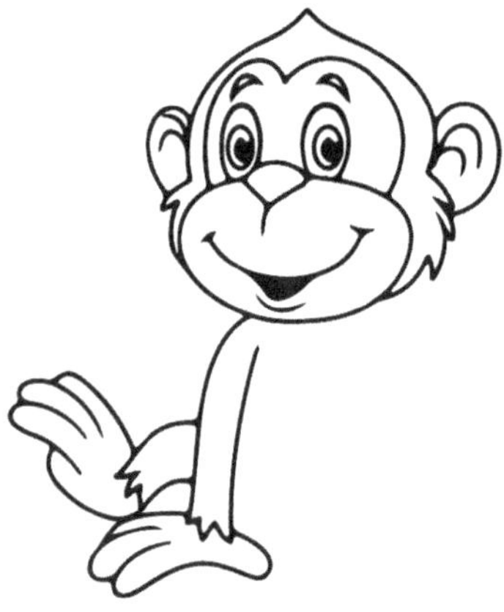

STEP - 5

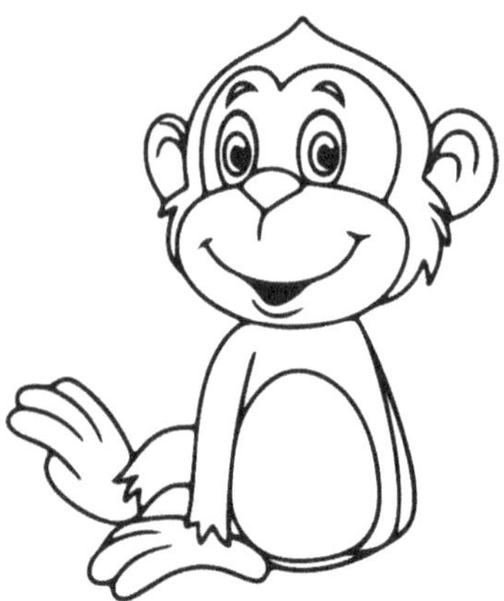

STEP - 6

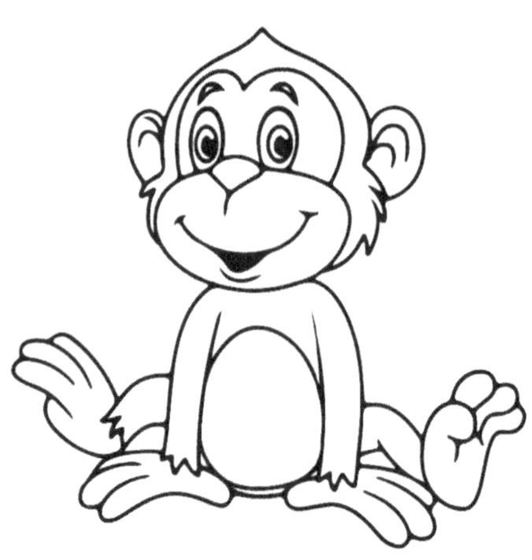

HOW TO DRAW

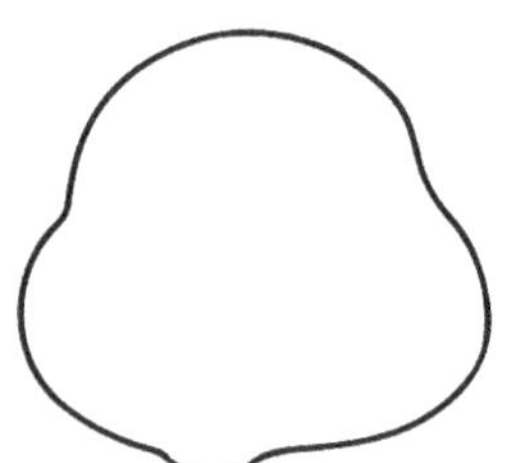

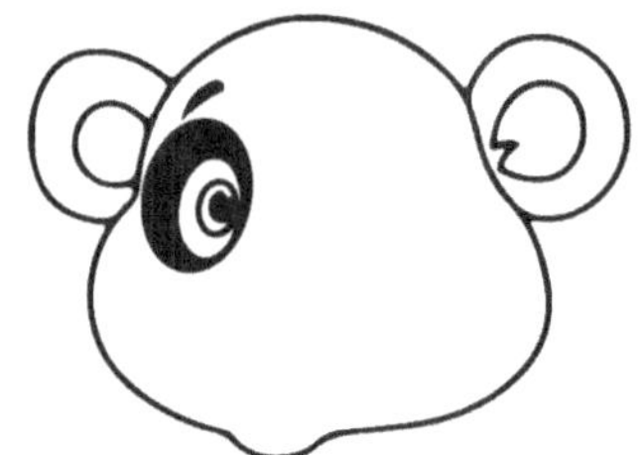

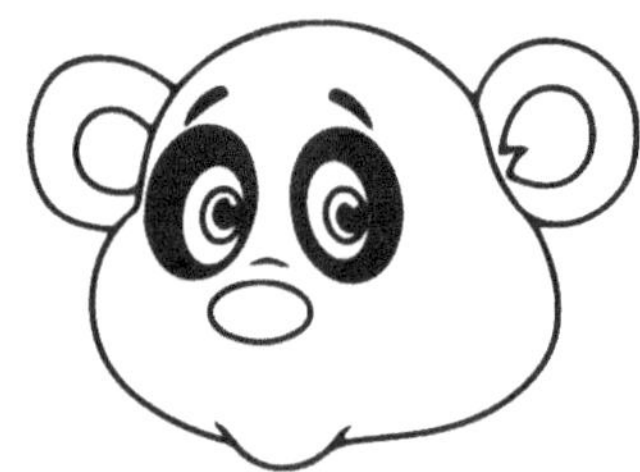

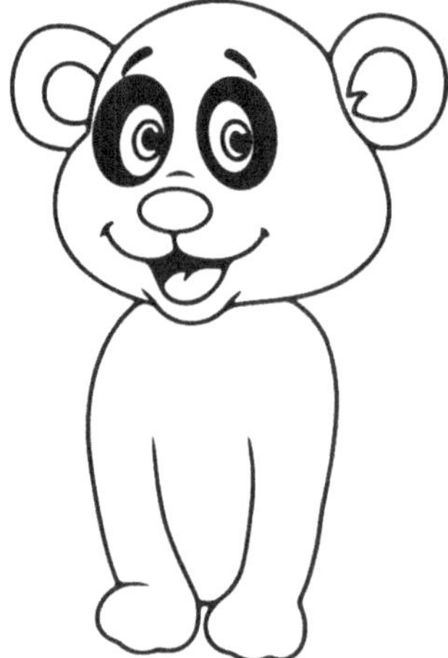

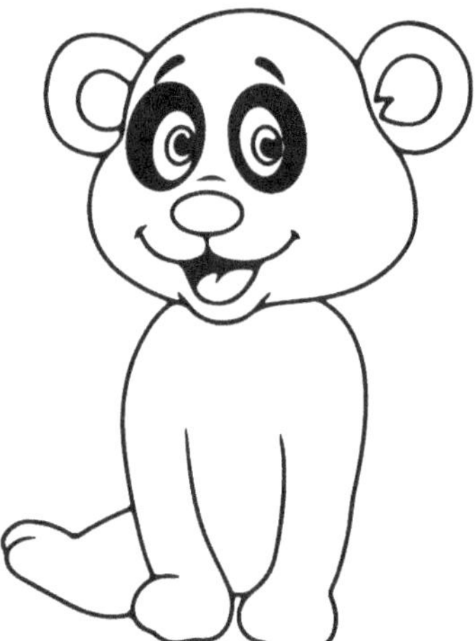

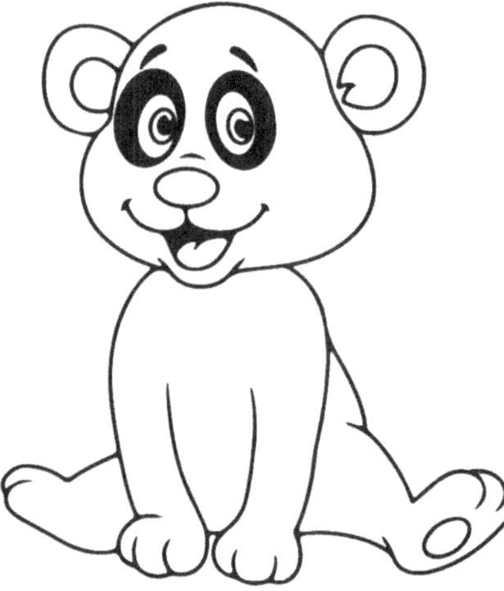

Your Test Pages

STEP - 1

STEP - 2

STEP - 3

STEP - 4

STEP - 5

STEP - 6

HOW TO DRAW

STEP - 1

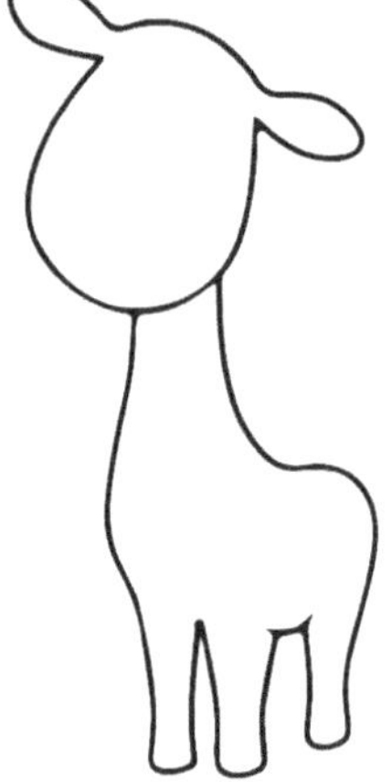

STEP - 2

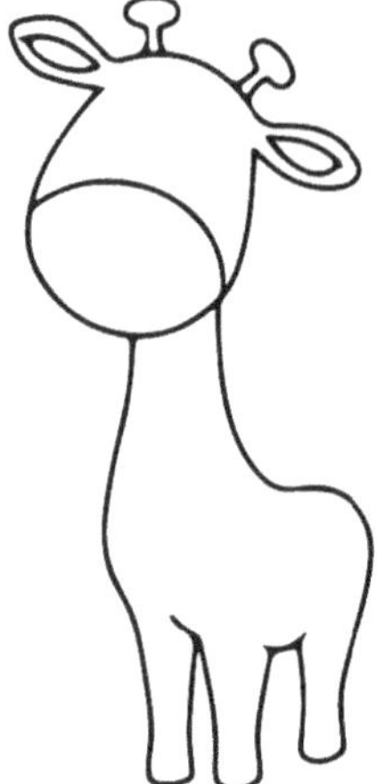

STEP - 3

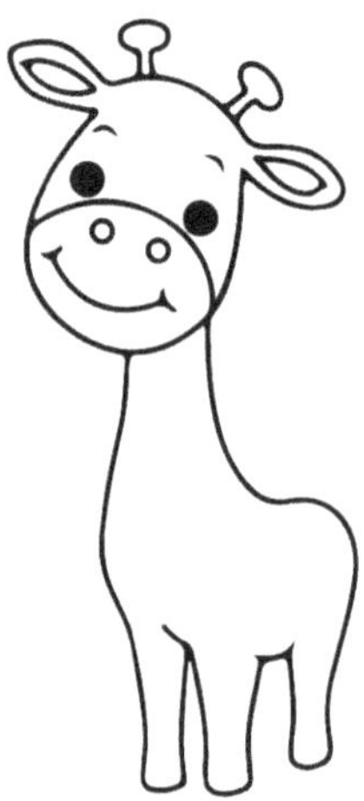

STEP - 4

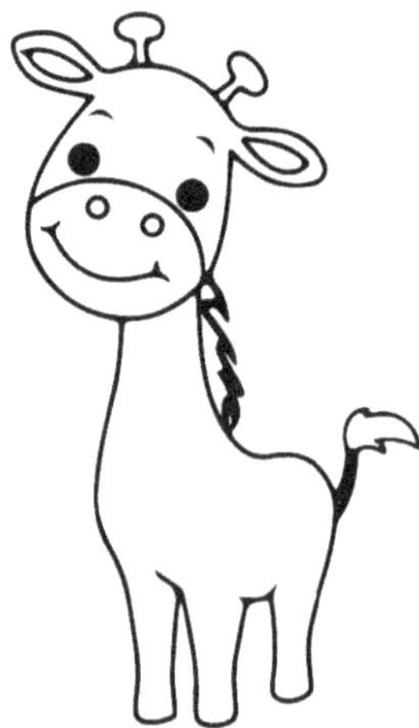

STEP - 5

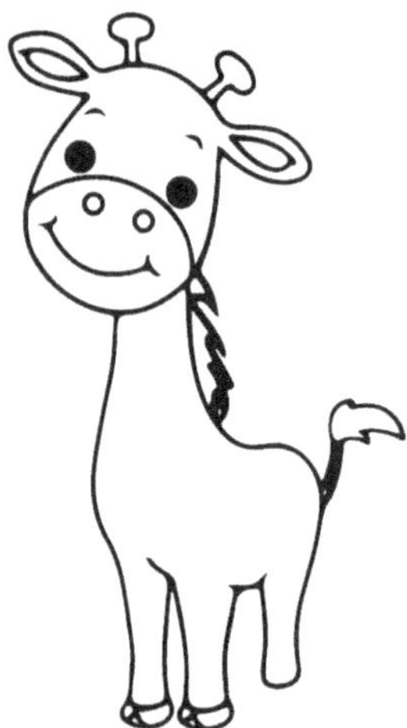

STEP - 6

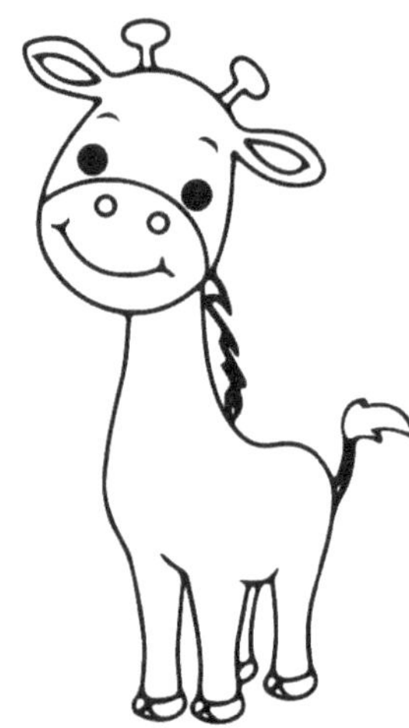

HOW TO DRAW

STEP - 1
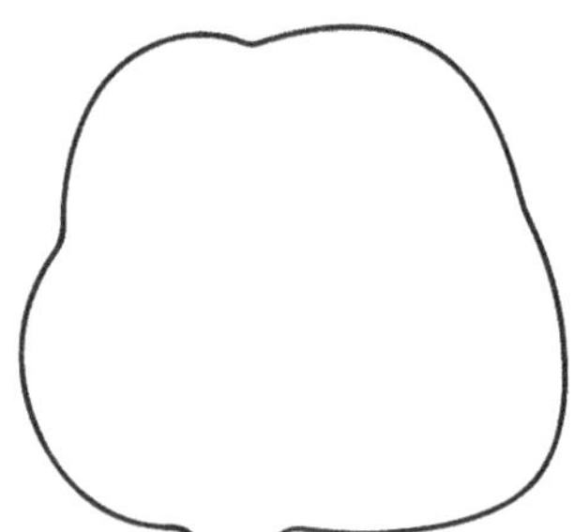

STEP - 2
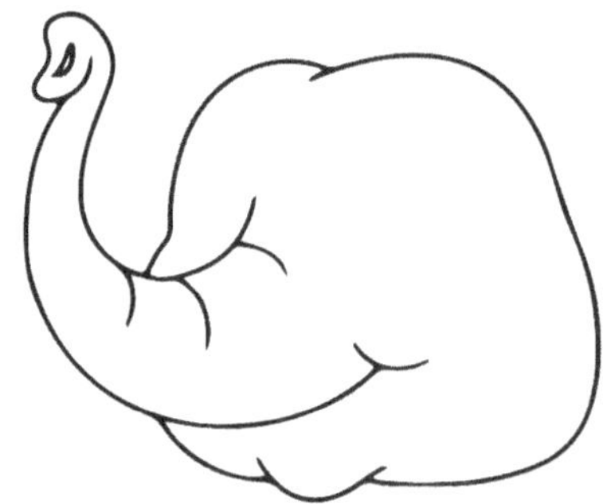

STEP - 3
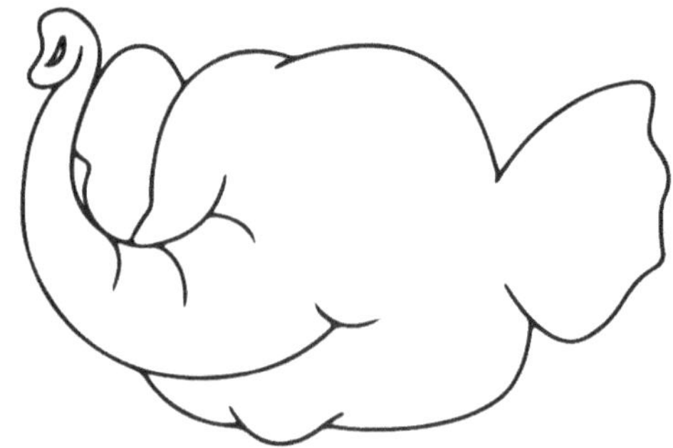

STEP - 4
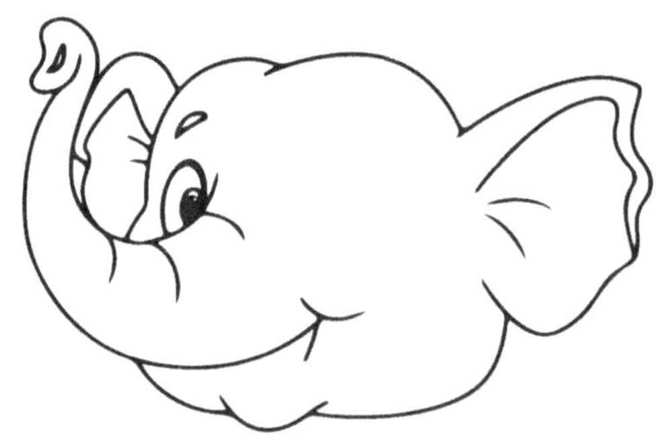

STEP - 5
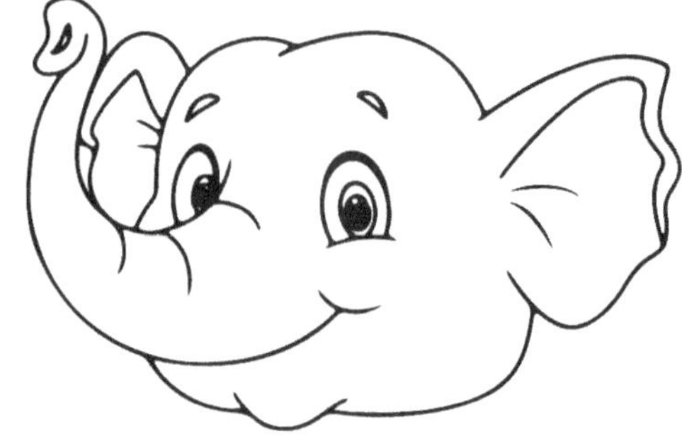

STEP - 6
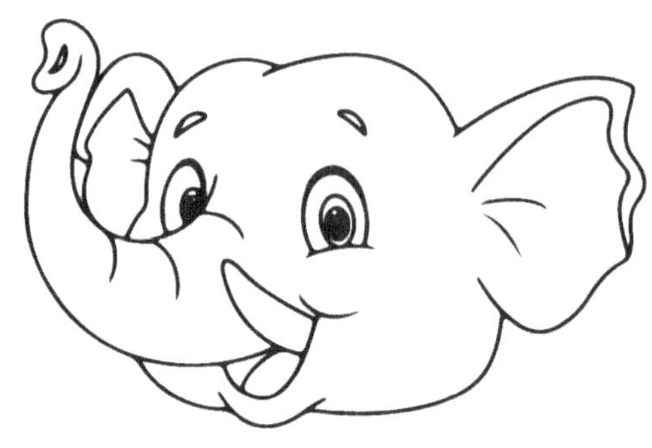

Your Test Pages

STEP - 1

STEP - 2

STEP - 3

STEP - 4

STEP - 5

STEP - 6